A Selected Bibliography of Applied Ethics
in the Professions, 1950–1970

Publications of the Graduate School of Business Administration
of the University of Virginia

A Selected Bibliography of
Applied Ethics in the Professions
1950-1970

A Working Sourcebook with Annotations and Indexes

Daniel L. Gothie

Graduate School of Business Administration,
University of Virginia

University Press of Virginia

Charlottesville

The publication of this study has been assisted by
the Center for the Study of Applied Ethics,
Graduate School of Business Administration,
University of Virginia

CONTENTS

FOREWORD

As the discussion in the first chapter points out, this collection assembles in one place the bibliographical data on books and articles of the last twenty years in many fields that focus on ethical implications of human behavior in specific situations. In some respects the items listed have little in common with each other, save the specifications set by the compiler. In short, cohesion is achieved in this volume more through the point of view used in putting it together than through the material itself.

One of the requirements for selection was publication during the interval 1950-1970. Admittedly, thinking and practice in many professions and fields of knowledge changed during these years. Certainly development will continue during the next twenty years. Thus what we have here is essentially an attempt to make available at a moment in time a considerable portion of what has been said by one generation; it is the approach of the snapshot or the balance sheet, with many of the same advantages and limitations.

Even casual scrutiny of the authors and titles included leads to a number of somewhat arresting conclusions. First, aside from the number of occupations and professions necessarily represented, the range and variety of the points of view, the ideologies, the politics of persons who have written in a given field are very great, almost extraordinary. No single school of thought or frame of reference, no set of specifics peculiar to one occupation has been able to preempt the field.

Second, and in part following from this first observation, the problem of defining what is or might or should be ethical behavior obviously extends across the whole spectrum of human activity-- irrespective of type of institution or form of economic or social organization. Critics of the free-enterprise and the free-market system notwithstanding, the difficulty of determining proper conduct is not confined to the profit-seeking sector of the economy. The same difficulty appears in the nonprofit sector. Indeed, in some ways it seems to bulk especially large in the professions (including the academic) in the government bureaucracy, in foundations, in trade unions, in all nonprofit institutions.

This line of thinking leads inevitably to consideration of the merits of a society entirely composed of nonprofit organizations, in which the profit motive is not needed or is used because society is controlled by the plans of "the best-qualified people," as well as to consideration of the relative merits of such a society as compared with one in which individual freedom of choice is the motivating force. As every adult in the second half of the twentieth century knows, down this road lie almost limitless speculation and debate.

Third, as one assesses the number and range of items in this collection and ponders their possible content, it seems clear that this problem is not one whose origin is neglect. There has been enough, perhaps more than enough research, thought, and writing, but too little agreement, adherence, and enforcement. This leads to a fourth observation.

Perhaps the difficulty in establishing accepted forms of conduct in large groups--such as the population of this country--stems in considerable measure from an absence of any substantial common background, common point of view, common scale of values, common understanding by individual persons of the society of which they form a part. Little in the literature of natural science, biology, or anthropology suggests that the confusion exemplified in this bibliography is a problem in an anthill or an aboriginal tribe.

Finally, if there is a common thread running through the several sections of the book, it may be the concern over conflict of interest in all the many guises it assumes in our modern, complicated, technological society, in which a single individual is permitted and often compelled to wear two or more hats. In a regimented economy, where the role of each person is circumscribed by higher authority and his responsibilities are adequately described by his social security number, where a family is most usefully defined as a consumption unit, the problem of conflict of interest is presumably greatly mitigated.

Considerations such as these raise a number of questions, though of course not the same questions for everyone. The following, however, may serve as a beginning. In view of the magnitude and the seriousness of the problems and complaints, implicit and explicit, discussed in the items listed here, how has modern society--particularly in the United States--managed to hang together at all? In studying such material as this volume contains, are we actually dealing with types of institutions and forms of social organization or with the frailties of human nature? Perhaps the psychologist and theologian may find common ground in asserting the latter to be the more probable hypothesis, but it seems unlikely that economists and social scientists will agree. Is conflict of interest the price we pay for economic and technological progress, and for political freedom?

Are there immutable truths that provide guidance in all these heterogeneous situations, or must the peculiarities of particular trades and organizations force their members to rely on themselves and their own special interests to set acceptable rules of conduct? This is an old conundrum, but the substance of this volume sharpens its present-day thrust, and one is reminded of the political adage that it is always easy to determine the right thing and always difficult to determine the truly expedient.

In the present turmoil and transformation of customs and morals in this country the great interest in proper behavior and ethical conduct is certainly an important, perhaps an inevitable, maybe even an optimistic aspect of the current scene. This bibliography, one of the first publications of the Center for the Study of Applied Ethics, provides a most useful reference point. Unquestionably it contributes to the public good, however this may be defined. The Center must be commended for the undertaking; it is hoped that the bibliography will be followed by a series of seminars, discussions, and monographs.

Pomfret, Connecticut
August 1972

Charles C. Abbott
Dean of the Graduate School of
  Business Administration (retired)
University of Virginia

THE CENTER FOR THE STUDY OF APPLIED ETHICS

Purpose

The Center for the Study of Applied Ethics has been established as an information and activities center to stimulate interest in and create awareness of operational ethical systems in various aspects of American life. More specifically, the Center exists for the following purposes:

1. to identify, define, and make explicit the nature and function of ethical systems and behavior in a free-enterprise environment;

2. to collect, analyze, and disseminate important concepts and data that exist in codes and ethical statements of formal public and private organizations, institutions, and professional groups;

3. to develop an institution that will provide a stimulating and supportive atmosphere conducive to the exchange of ethical ideas and concepts between businessmen, public officials, community leaders, nonprofit organizations, members of the professions, members of academic communities and other interested parties.

4. to provide guidance and support for research and publication in the area of applied ethics, both in the public and private sectors of our society.

In conjunction with the Library of the Graduate School of Business Administration of the University of Virginia, the Center for the Study of Applied Ethics collects and maintains a data base of materials on ethics, ethical behavior, and ethical systems. This data base is available to all interested individuals or organizations for use in study or research involving applied ethics.

Another function of the Center is the development of educational programs such as lectures, seminars, forums, and courses to provide a continuing discourse on applied ethics. As part of this program, the Center is responsible for the establishment of a professional chair named in honor of the founders of the Center, Elis and Signe Olsson.

History

In 1966 Mrs. Elis M. Olsson established a trust in memory of her late husband to provide an endowed professorial chair at the University of Virginia. The Board of Visitors of the University of Virginia in turn authorized the Elis and Signe Olsson Professorship in the Graduate School of Business Administration, noting the donor's intent as focusing on

> the enormous importance of integrity in
> human affairs . . . . to stimulate general
> public interest in and understanding of the
> ethical implications that necessarily adhere
> to the exercise of authority in both public
> and private life . . . . aim at attaining a
> position of leadership, in efforts to improve
> standards of behavior in both public and
> private business . . . emphasize the
> essentiality of integrity in the reconcilia-
> tion of those concepts commonly indicated
> as the dignity of the individual, the im-
> peratives of organizations and the moral-
> ities implicit in free markets.

During the next three years, under the leadership of Dean Charles C. Abbott of the Graduate School of Business Administration, a variety of interested people, including University of Virginia faculty, representative leaders of the business community, and Graduate School of Business Administration Sponsor Trustees, worked together to formulate concrete plans to carry out the intentions of the Olsson Trust.

In the spring of 1969 a prospectus for a Center for the Study of Applied Ethics was sent to President Edgar F. Shannon for approval. President Shannon's authorization of the Center came on May 7, and adoption of an official charter for the Center followed on May 15 of the same year.

Professor Alexander B. Horniman of the Graduate School of Business Administration became the first executive director for the CSAE shortly after the charter was adopted. During the summer of 1969, Dr. Horniman and Dean Abbott developed an advisory council to provide guidance to the Center. The advisory council met in January 1970 in Charlottesville to set tentative plans for Center activities and to determine organizational relationships. From this meeting came the initial efforts of the Center: (1) development of a bibliography on ethics, (2) a research project to identify areas for further exploration, and (3) a major seminar entitled "Are Ethical Considerations Relevant in Time of Changing Values?" These first projects exemplify the continuing activities of the Center.

Future Plans

As an extension of its early programs and in line with its stated purpose, the Center for the Study of Applied Ethics will actively seek to implement additional seminars and forums in the near future, focusing on current ethical issues. As an adjunct, plans call for the publication of the Center's activities in issue-oriented monographs and of its data base as bibliographies. Interested parties are invited to contact the Center for additional information or as potential participants in the Center's work and activities.

CLASSIFICATION AND ORGANIZATION
OF THE BIBLIOGRAPHY

This bibliography is a selected reference guide and source book of information on applied ethics in the professions. It covers the period from 1950 to 1970 and is comprised of materials in English, primarily those published in the United States. For works available for review, brief descriptive annotations have been made. The major part of the bibliography includes books, monographs, and periodical articles as well as important pamphlets, unpublished speeches, and miscellaneous materials.

The purposes of this work are twofold: it is intended, first, to serve as a working data base for the Center for the Study of Applied Ethics, and, second, to present sources of pertinent information on ethical behavior in the professions for the use of all interested parties. It is hoped that this bibliography will be used as a working source-book, to be amended, expanded, and revised at intervals of five years, with important useful supplements issued as they are developed by the Center. Any interested parties who wish to contribute to the continuing progress of this bibliography are invited to contact the author at the Center for the Study of Applied Ethics.

Toward a Definition of Applied Ethics

At the very least, "applied ethics" is a vague expression. As defined by the Center for the Study of Applied Ethics, the phrase refers to ethical or moralistic behavior as observed in actual practice by institutions, groups, and individuals under societal conditions rather than in unilateral, individualistic situations. In opposition to a philosophical approach to ethics and moral decision-making, applied ethics constitutes action and reaction to established circumstances, guidelines, rules, regulations, laws, and codes of society, established in the sense that they are commonly accepted or understood as behavioral standards.

More specifically, applied ethical behavior encompasses deviations from or adherence to accepted practices, either by individuals or by organized groups. The codification of behavioral standards as formal and informal canons and rules is also included in our definition of applied ethics. Then again, the phrase encompasses controversies over developing and enforcing codes and regulations. It also concerns itself with changes in attitude as well as in observed behavioral patterns. In general, applied ethics emphasizes ethical behavior in action rather than ethical contemplation or logic.

It follows from this rather simplistic definition that "applied ethics" is used here as a record of ethical behavior rather than as a dialogue. Perhaps the recording of ethical behavior and of changes in ethical behavior will contribute to understanding motivations of those individuals and institutions involved in the everyday mechanics of our society.

The Professions

Reference to the professions means those societal groups whose common interest has led them to make formal the interrelationships of their individual members. For a variety of purposes, Americans seem to be obsessed with the formation of associations, organizations, and formal groups. Those referred to here are ones representing specially trained individuals whose skills are not easily acquired and whose actions in the practice of their skills are subject to a high degree of public and private scrutiny, regulation, and/or reaction.

Professions are defined here as law, medicine, engineering, business, government, the sciences, education, politics, and health professions such as psychiatry, public health, and nursing. While argument over the validity of these categories as professions continues, this bibliography will consider the ethical concerns of these areas. One noticeable absence is that of religion, long established as a professional activity in this country. Suffice it to say that the religious concentration on theological and philosophical problems exempts it from consideration except in materials fitting our definition of applied ethics.

Scope and Arrangement of the Bibliography

In view of the rise of the modern technological society following World War II and the stress placed on social behavior during the period by more rapid rates of change, the time span 1950 to 1970 was chosen as making a valuable contribution to the record of changing ethical attitudes. Only those materials identified as being published in and after 1950 have been entered in this work.

Arranged in alphabetical order by professional areas, the sections of this work are further subdivided where there are clear divisions within an area of professional activity. For instance, the Business and Management section contains a list of works pertaining to general commentary on ethics in business plus separate lists related to ethical practices in accounting, finance, marketing, and other subfields. In the Government and Politics section, it was easier to follow a geographic classification, paralleling governmental structure and associated political activity.

This bibliography was conceived originally as a work that would concentrate mainly on three professions: law, medicine, and business management. It soon became obvious that the intended objectives of the Center for the Study of Applied Ethics would require materials from other areas of endeavor as well, and the scope of the bibliography was expanded to cover the natural, physical and social sciences, engineering, government and politics, and related fields. Material written on ethics in each of these areas varied considerably as to media and to the extent of the discourse within the field.

General Trends in Professional Fields

During the compilation of the bibliographic references in each of the categories, certain patterns of ethical trends within each professional area emerged. These trends and further details of the bibliographic organization are described below.

Business and Management. This section begins with a list of general references that serve as additional sources of bibliographic data or reading lists. Included are major codes of conduct or regulations established by official or quasi-official associations or organizations. The next subdivision covers works pertaining to general business activities or ethical behavior. Following this major section are briefer sections on accounting, advertising, finance, labor and personnel, production, marketing, and religion and business. Their brevity reflects ethical concern on a plane higher than that of the market place.

Issues that received most emphasis in this literature were those concerned primarily with the social effects of individual business actions. The current emphasis on consumer protection and social responsibilities represents the culmination of twenty years' interest in business behavior in a social context. Three cases of deviation from legal or social rules figure among the examples during this period: the Billy Sol Estes affair, the General Electric price-fixing scandal, and the Great Salad Oil Swindle. Generally, the literature reflects growing pressure for greater public protection and establishment of standards rather than debate over the rights or wrongs of particular situations.

Engineering. The engineering section is divided into two parts, the first consisting of the few identifiable books and references available, and a longer segment of journal articles and codes representing the bulk of literature on engineering ethics.

As a professional calling, engineering emerges as a tighter community than business, perhaps by nature of the scientific training and discipline of its practitioners. The literature mainly debates three problems: the question of technological development and social impact, the conduct of engineering consultants, and the integrity of privileged information in job mobility. Associations in the engineering field appear to have some degree of influence in guiding professional behavior, but are not as authoritative as those in medicine and law.

General Ethical Philosophy. This section consists of a selected reading list in the area of ethical philosophy and is intended to offer background material leading up to examination of applied ethics in modern society. Hardly an all-inclusive list, this segment, headed by several representative bibliographies and compendiums, only represents a highly subjective choice of those materials that aim ethical philosophy at applied ethical situations.

Government and Politics. As might be expected, the Federal Government maintains a vested interest in the behavior of its working parts. This is mirrored in the bibliographies and references at the beginning of this section, all prepared by the U.S. Library of Congress Legislative Reference Service. The remainder of the section comprises four parts, one each on federal, state, local governments and ethics, and the last on political philosophy and ethical behavior.

Clearly the major ethical problems facing government officials and politicians have been conflict of interest between public and private desires, regulatory integrity, and public responsibility. The literature of government codes at various levels and the barbs of the press aimed at alleged misconduct serve to underscore these concerns.

Health Sciences. Again, this section starts with useful references on ethical principles and practices in medical and other health professions. Of major significance as a source of medical ethical literature is Irving Ladimer's Clinical Investigation in Medicine; Legal, Ethical and Moral Aspects. A variety of books, addresses, articles, and editorial reports on the medical profession follows, with brief segments on nursing, psychiatry, and other health professions such as public health, psychology, and pharmacology.

In fashion similar to law, the medical profession has a taut organizational structure, headed by the august American Medical Association. But, despite the frequent issuance of principles, guidelines, procedures, ethical codes, opinions, and medicolegal advice, the medical profession confronts a continuing controversy in the question of life-death decisions. Stemming from that overriding issue is the one faced in development of, experimentation with, and application of new drugs and techniques. Concern with this persistent issue pervades the literature of medical ethics to the point of obscuring relatively rare discussions of fee-splitting and malpractice. That this concern may change is possible, with the increasing incidence of malpractice suits, but it seems a positive focal point until medical technological advances diminish.

Law. Three major areas constitute the body of legal ethical literature. The first includes official codes, canons, and principles of ethical practice formulated and promulgated by official legal associations, primarily the American Bar Association. A second part covers books, periodical articles, and miscellaneous material on a variety of legal ethical subjects. The final segment lists similar materials on medical-legal relationships.

A major difficulty with ethics in the legal profession is enforcing ethical practices. With fairly tight licensing standards, relatively clear-cut standards of practice, and a close community organization, lawyers are often reluctant to prosecute violators of their own codes and tend to protect the general public image of the legal profession. Ethical literature in this field then deals mainly with establishment of specific guidelines and with new developments such as the increasing rate of malpractice suits and civil liberties activities.

Science. Once more, bibliographies introduce the main body of literature on science and ethical behavior. At the end, the third part of this section deals with science and its influence on public policy. A majority of the works cited are from scientific journals rather than in more codified form.

In discussing the scientific community here, the reference is primarily to natural and physical sciences, although the overall scientific community is often under consideration. Unlike the more formal professions of law and medicine, science allies individuals and groups from a spectrum of disciplines and subdisciplines whose most common interest is the pursuit and discovery of truth and knowledge. Ethical involvement of scientists, as reflected in the literature, is usually in the form of massive reaction to misapplications or failures of scientific discoveries. Misgivings over the atomic bomb and other military weaponry have yielded to greater ecological concern over the rate and mismanagement of technological progress in recent years.

<u>Social Sciences</u>. For the last chapter, the literature of the social sciences and ethics was divided as follows: bibliographies and references, general works, economics, education, history and narrative comment, psychology, and sociology. These fields all seemed to have functioning societal activities that fit our definition of applied ethics and sufficient literary discourse on ethical behavior and practice to merit inclusion, the professionalism of any of them notwithstanding.

This category represents something of a catchall for thought and debate on our society's complex interrelationships and activities. Perhaps the only distinguishing feature of ethics literature in the social sciences is its exaggerated efforts towards the improvement of the human condition.

Bibliographic Form and Sources

Since the citations in this book originated from a broad variety of sources, some effort was made to standardize bibliographic form, particularly for journal articles, which are often cited quite differently between the sciences and humanities. In certain cases, the lack of descriptive bibliographic data precluded consideration of materials that might have been useful. Generally, the form used follows the format cited in <u>A Manual of Style</u>, 12th ed. (Chicago: University of Chicago Press, 1969).

Every effort has been made to be consistent in this format throughout the bibliography despite the appearance of many exceptions or problem entries.

Sources for bibliographic listings included bibliographies in existence, references in pertinent literature, the ethics collection of the Center for the Study of Applied Ethics, materials sent in by interested parties, the National Union Catalogue, publishers' catalogue, and a number of library card catalogues. Within reasonable time limits, most works referenced in this bibliography were checked against the National Union Catalogue or were verified by sight.

A Selected Bibliography of Applied Ethics
in the Professions, 1950–1970

BUSINESS AND MANAGEMENT

Bibliographies and References

Bartels, Robert, ed. Ethics in Business. Columbus: Ohio State University Press, 1963.
   This book of readings by prominent business authorities covers most functional areas in the field and includes an extensive bibliography.

Baumhart, Raymond. An Honest Profit: What Businessmen Say About Ethics in Business. New York: Holt, Rinehart & Winston, 1968.
   A classic study of top management attitudes toward ethical business behavior, this analysis is a rarity in its attempt to give ethics a mathematical dimension.

Masterson, Thomas R., comp. Ethics in Business. Ed. T. R. Masterson and S. Carlton Numan. New York: Pitman, 1968.
   An anthology of contemporary comments on ethical regulation of business and economic activities, including sections on self-regulation of business and current problems in business ethics. Suggested research and readings are proposed in the final section.

Van Vlack, Philip W. Management Ethics Guide. Bulletin 523. Brookings: South Dakota State University, 1964.
   This work offers a practical approach to business ethics and a brief bibliography of major works in the field.

_____, Charles L. Sewrey, and Charles E. Nielsen. Economics Ethics Bibliography. Brookings: South Dakota State University, 1964.
   Annotated listing of business and economics literature pertaining to ethics and ethical behavior.

General Works

American Academy of Political and Social Sciences. The Ethics of Business Enterprise. Ed. Arthur S. Miller. Philadelphia: American Academy of Political and Social Sciences, 1962.

American Management Association. A Collection of Some Representative Documents Involving in Varying Degrees Application of Ethical Principles of Business Programs. New York: American Management Association, 1962.

Anthony, Robert N. "The Trouble with Profit Maximization." Harvard Business Review 38 (Nov.-Dec. 1960): 126-34.

Appley, Lawrence A. "Oh Ye of Little Faith." Management News 36 (Apr. 1963).

Austin, Robert W. "Code of Conduct for Executives." Harvard Business Review 39 (Sept.-Oct. 1961): 53-61.

_____. "Who Has the Responsibility for Social Change-- Business or Government?" Harvard Business Review 43 (July-Aug. 1965): 45-52.

Baily, Nathan A. "The Role of Business and Business School in Raising Ethical Standards in Business." MSU Business Topics (Michigan State University) 5 (spring,1968): 29-32.

Barnard, Chester Irving. "Elementary Conditions of Business Morals." California Management Review 1 (fall, 1958): 1-13.

_____. Elementary Conditions of Business Morals. Berkeley: University of California Press, 1958.

Baum, Maurice, ed. Readings in Business Ethics: A Survey of the Principles and Problems of American Business Morality. Dubuque, Iowa: William C. Brown, 1951.

Bennett, John C. Outlaws in Swivel Chairs. New York: Comet
    Press Books [1958].

Bennion, Francis Alan Roscoe. Professional Ethics: The Consultant
Professions and Their Code. London: C. Knight, 1969.

Bensman, Joseph. Dollars and Sense. New York: Macmillan,
1967.
    Comparative study of advertising as a profit-oriented pro-
fession with the academic world as a nonprofit profession. Con-
cludes with an analysis of the meaning of work in its personal and
social setting.

Berrigan, Daniel. Consequences: Truth and . . . . New York:
Macmillan, 1967.

Boulding, Kenneth E., Carl Sherman Voss, and Walter A. Kaufman.
Ethics and Business: Three Lectures. University Park, Pa.: 1962.

Bowen, Howard R. Social Responsibilities of the Businessman. New
York: Harper & Brothers, 1953.

Braun, Carl F. Fair Thought and Speech. 5th ed. Alhambra, Calif.:
C. F. Braun & Co., 1957.

Brayman, Harold. Corporate Management in a World of Politics.
New York: McGraw-Hill, 1967.

Brennan, Lawrence David. The Concept of Business Ethics Reflected
in America's Literary Awakening, 1820-1835. Ann Arbor, Mich.:
University Microfilms, 1950.

Broehl, Wayne G., Jr. "Insights into Business and Society" Harvard
Business Review 44 (May-June 1966): 6-15.

-4-

Bunting, James Whitney, et al., eds. Ethics for Modern Business
Practice. New York: Prentice-Hall, 1953.

"Business Gifts: Who Pays the Bill?" Dun's Review and Modern
Industry 67 (Nov. 1960).

Can, A. F. "Can an Executive Afford a Conscience?" Harvard Business
Review 48 (July 1970): 58-64.

Carle, J. Francis. "Let's Talk About Your Ethics." Administrative
Management 23 (May 1963).

Cary, William L. "The Case for Higher Corporate Standards." Harvard
Business Review 40 (Sept.-Oct. 1962).

Cheit, Earl F. "Why Managers Cultivate Social Responsibility."
California Management Review 6 (fall, 1964): 3-22.

Childs, Marquis William and Douglass Cater. Ethics in a Business
Society. New York: Harper & Brothers, 1954.
        An investigation into the relationship between religion and
American economic life, searching for an answer to the question of
the role of the individual and a balance between morality and business
responsibilities.

Clason, George Samuel, comp. The Richest Man in Babylon. New
York: Hawthorn Books, 1955.

"A Code for Industrial Purchasing." Advanced Management Journal 25
(Apr. 1961).

"Code of Conduct for Executives." Harvard Business Review 39
(Sept.-Oct. 1961).

"Code of Ethics." Agent and Representative 16 (Nov. 1965).

-5-

"Code of Ethics." Industrial Security 8 (Oct. 1965).

Cole, Arthur H. Business Enterprise in Its Social Setting. Cambridge,
Mass.: Harvard University Press, 1959.

Collier, A. T. "Social Responsibilities of the Businessman." Management Review 34 (July 1957).

"Corporate Directorship Practices," in Studies in Business Policy
No. 125. New York: National Industrial Conference Board, 1967.
pp. 108-125.

Decker, James A., ed. The Good Business Treasure Chest. New York:
Hawthorne Books, 1958.

Dent, James K. Organizational Correlates of the Goals of Business
Managements. Ann Arbor: University of Michigan & Wayne State
University, in Journal of Personnel Psychology, August, 1959.

Dewey, Orville. Moral Views of Commerce, Society and Politics in
Twelve Discourses. New York: Augustus M. Kelley, 1969.

Drucker, Peter F. "Big Business and the National Purpose." Harvard
Business Review 40 (Mar.-Apr. 1962).

_____. The New Society. New York: Harper & Brothers,
1950.
    Drucker concludes that this nation needs greater encourage-
ment for enterprise and individual initiative in business because of
the problems and disorder created by the growth of our major business
corporations and institutions. He deals mainly with problems and
principles of industrial order, which is really the consideration of
rational social policies by business.

Eckel, Malcolm W. The Ethics of Decision Making. New York:
Morehouse-Barlow, 1968.
    A short case study book citing twelve specific situations
involving ethical problems and considerations.

_____. The Meaning of Modern Business. New York:
Columbia University Press, 1960.
Defines the modern corporation and problems involving the
development of an adequate philosophical framework for corporate
responsibilities as these have been understood in the past several
decades.

Eells, Richard. "Beyond the Golden Rule." Columbia Journal of World
Business 2 (July-Aug. 1967): 82-88.
Says business ethics are for industrial, as distinct from corporate,
morality for the corporation. Refers to Barnard on conflict of moralities:
"Corporation is a multifunctional major social institution."

_____, and Clarence Walton. Conceptual Foundations of
Business. Homewood, Ill.: Richard D. Irwin, 1961.
A broad-brush treatment of business operations considered in
terms of the basic pillars of Western society: freedom, ownership,
the market economy, constitutionalism, progress. Extensive suggested reading lists after each section provide bibliographic direction.

Elbing, Alvar O., and Carol L. Elbing. The Value Issue of Business.
New York: McGraw-Hill, 1967.
Based on the "implicit social value assumptions of classical
economics," this book attempts to formulate a systematic framework
for analysis of the value issue of business. Short bibliography and
references after each chapter.

Ellis, W. W., Jr., and K. D. Beck. "New Law Clarifies Treatment of
Fines, Penalties, Bribes and Anti-Trust Payments." Journal of Taxation
32 (May 1970): 276-77.

"Ensuring Ethical Conduct in Business." Conference Board Record 25
(Dec. 1964): 17ff.

Eppert, Ray R. "Corporate Policy as a Code of Ethical Conduct: Moral
Basis for Business Leadership." Management Record (Mar. 1962).

"The Ethical Dilemmas of Businessmen." Challenge 4 (Jan. 1962).

"Ethics for Today's Business Society." Controller 29 (Apr. 1961).

"Ethics in Business." Advanced Management Journal 29 (Apr. 1965):
14-20.

The Ethics of American Business. Princeton, N.J.: Opinion Research
Corporation, 1964.
    Results of personal interviews with a nationwide sample of the
American public and of questionnaires sent to leading business execu-
tives on business attitudes and practices.

The Ethics of Business: Corporate Behavior in the Market Place.
New York: Columbia Graduate School of Business, 1963.
    A symposium conducted at the Columbia Graduate School of
Business. Introduction by Courtney C. Brown. Participants: Philip
Sporn, Lean F. Hickman, and Luther H. Hodges. An appendix contains
a statement on business ethics by the Business Ethics Advisory Council.

"The Ethics of Business Enterprise." Annals of the American Academy
of Political and Social Science 71 (Sept. 1962): 1-141.

"Existentialism for the Businessman." Harvard Business Review 38
(Mar.-Apr. 1960).

Finkelstein, Louis. "The Businessman's Moral Failure." Fortune 28
(Sept. 1958): 116-17ff.

Fitzpatrick, George D. "Good Business and Good Ethics." Advanced
Management Journal 30 (Oct. 1965): 23-28.

Flubach, Joseph Francis. The Concept of Ethics in the History of
Economics. New York: Vantage Press, 1950.

Fulmer, P. M. "Ethical Codes for Business." Personnel Administration
32 (May 1969): 49-57.

-8-

Fulmer, Robert M. An Investigation into the Ethical Standards of
Graduating M.B.A.'s. Tallahassee: Florida State University, 1967.

Galbraith, John Kenneth. The Affluent Society. Boston: Houghton
Mifflin, 1958.

Garrett, Thomas M. Business Ethics. New York: Appleton-Century-
Crofts, 1966.

_____. Ethics in Business. New York: Sheed & Ward,
1963.

Geis, G., ed. White Collar Criminal:--The Offender in Business and
the Professions. New York: Atherton, 1968.

Gelinier, O. The Enterprise Ethic. London: Institute of Economic
Affairs, 1968.

Gilman, Glenn. "The Ethical Dimension in American Management."
California Management Review 7 (fall, 1964): 45-52.

Glover, J. D. The Attack on Big Business. Boston: Harvard Business
School, 1954.

Gluch, Samuel E. The Ethical Development of Managerial Responsibility.
New York: Columbia University Press, 1960.

Golden, L. L. L. Only by Public Consent: American Corporations
Search for Favorable Opinion. New York: Hawthorn Books, 1968.

Golembiewski, Robert T. Men, Management and Morality: Toward a
New Organizational Ethic. New York: McGraw-Hill, 1965.

Graham, G. "Answer to Corruption." Nation's Business 57 (Sept.
1969): 46-49.

Greenwood, William T., ed. Issues in Business and Society: Readings and Cases. Boston: Houghton Mifflin, 1964.

Guertler, C. B. "Written Standards of Ethics in Purchasing." Journal of Purchasing 4 (May 1968): 46-51.

Guth, William D., and Renato Tagiuri. "Personal Values and Corporate Strategy." Harvard Business Review 34 (Sept.-Oct. 1965).

Hagen, Willis W. "Ethics in Business." Advanced Management Journal 20 (Apr. 1965): 14-20.

Harvard Business Review. "Ethics for Executives Series." Cambridge, Mass.: Harvard University Press, 1968.

"Have Corporations a Higher Duty than Profits?" Fortune 31 (Aug. 1960).

Hay, Robert D. "A Proposed Code of Ethics for Business Administration Educators." Advance Management 26 (Sept. 1961).

Hayne, Paul T. Private Keepers of the Public Interest. New York: McGraw-Hill, 1967.
    A critique of businessmen's attitudes towards social responsibilities that encourages the businessman to accept a code encompassing a higher sense of self-esteem as the basis for improved business ethics.

Hodges, Luther Hartwell. The Business Conscience. Englewood Cliffs, N.J.: Prentice-Hall, 1963.

_____. "The Gray Area in Business Ethics." Management Review 41 (Mar. 1963).

Houser, T. V. Big Business and Human Values. New York: McGraw-Hill, 1957.

"How Ethical Are Businessmen?" Management Accounting 50 (Jan. 1969): 63-64.

"Industry's Ethics Could Be Better." Space/Aeronautics 39 (Mar. 1963): 114.

International Conference on Control of Restrictive Business Practices, Chicago, 1958. Proceedings. Glencoe: Ill.: Free Press for Graduate School of Business, University of Chicago, 1960.

"Is Business Bluffing Ethical?" Harvard Business Review 47 (Jan.-Feb. 1968): 143ff.

Jaspers, K. Future of Mankind. Chicago: University of Chicago Press, 1961.

Johnston, Herbert. Business Ethics. 2nd rev. ed. New York: Pitman, 1961.
        Logical definition of ethical behavior and guiding privileges, including supplementary case studies. Organization of the book is mainly by functional areas of business activity, i.e., labor, government, ethical behavior, capital.

"Keeping a High Shine on Ethics." Business Week 33 (Mar. 25, 1961).

Kuhn, James W. "What's Wrong with the Old Business Ethic?" Columbia University Forum 8 (summer, 1964): 22-26.

_____, and Ivan Berg. Values in a Business Society: Issues and Analyses. New York: Harcourt, Brace & World, 1968.
        Based on Columbia University's Business School course Conceptual Foundations of Business, this work covers major aspects of the business environment from the labor-business confrontation through governmental regulation to the role of the individual in the corporate world. Numerous examples and leading questions set the stage for further analysis by students and researchers.

Langdale, Noah, Jr. "Ethics and the Businessman." NADA Magazine 47 (Mar. 1963).

Learned, Edmund P. "Personal Values and Business Decisions." Harvard Business Review 38 (Mar.-Apr. 1959).

Levitt, Theodore. "The Dangers of Social Responsibility." Harvard Business Review 37 (Sept.-Oct. 1958).

Leys, Wayne A. R. Ethics for Policy Decisions: The Art of Asking Deliberative Questions. Englewood Cliffs, N.J.: Prentice-Hall, 1962.
    Utilizes a review of classic philosophical issues as a framework for approaching policy issues, then examines such broad-scale examples as TVA and the partition of Germany. Extensively referenced and indexed.

Lilienthal, David E. Big Business: A New Era. New York: Harper & Row, 1952.

"Low Marks in Ethics." Business Week 40 (Sept. 28, 1968): 64ff.
    A Stanford Business School seminar reveals that students there have a low opinion of businessmen's ethical behavior.

Lynes, Russell. The Tastemakers. New York: Grosset & Dunlap, 1954.
    Historical account of the basis for taste in families of American professional men, primarily lawyers and businessmen.

"Making an Honest Buck." Nation's Business 56 (Aug. 1958): 84ff.

Management and Growth:--Management's Creative Task of a World of Increasing Complexity and Accelerated Growth. Fourteeneth International Management Congress of Conseil International pour l'Organisation Scientifique, Rotterdam, Sept. 19-23, 1967. Rotterdam: University Press, 1967.

Mason, Edward S. "The Apologetics of Managerialism." Journal of Business 31 (Jan. 1958): 1-11.

_____, ed. The Corporation in Modern Society. Cambridge, Mass.: Harvard University Press, 1959.
  A collection of exceptional essays on the American corporate system, manifested in its external appearance relative to other economic factors such as law, unions, politics, and technology.

Masters, Josephine. "The Apologetics of Managerialism." Journal of Business 31 (Jan. 1958): 1-11.

Masterson, Thomas R., comp. Ethics in Business. Ed. T. R. Masterson and S. Carlton Nunan. New York: Pitman, 1968.
  An anthology of contemporary comments on ethical regulation of business and economic activities, including sections on self-regulation and current problems in business ethics. Suggested research and readings are proposed in the final section.

Mathes, Sorrel M., and G. Clark Thompson. "Ensuring Ethical Conduct in Business." Conference Board Record (National Industrial Conference Board) 26 (Dec. 1964): 17-27.

Meggison, L. C. "Ethical Standards of Conduct of Business." Advanced Management Journal 25 (May 1960).

Michelman, Irving S. Business at Bay: Critics and Heretics of American Business. New York: Augustus M. Kelley, 1969.
  Study of Veblen, Lewis, Eccles, Quinn, Eaton, Berle, Harrington, and Marcuse as dissenters from the traditional views of American business.

Miller, Samuel H. "The Tangle of Ethics." Harvard Business Review 39 (Jan.-Feb. 1960).

Mohan, R. P. Technology and Christian Culture. Washington, D.C.: Catholic University of America Press, 1960.

"Must Designers Choose Between Ethics and Survival?" Engineering News 180 (May 16, 1968): 26-7.

Nader, Ralph. Unsafe at Any Speed: The Designed-in Dangers of the American Automobile. New York: Grossman, 1965.
     This famous attack on the automobile industry's failure to provide adequate collision protection and other safety devices is now a classic.

National Association of Manufacturers. Manual of Official Policy Positions. New York: National Association of Manufacturers, 1969.

"New Goals for Business Ethics." Steel 81 (Mar. 26, 1962).

Norris, Louis William. "Moral Hazards of an Executive." Harvard Business Review 39 (Sept.-Oct. 1960): 72-79.

Northwood Institute. Corporate Policy and Ethics. Washington, D.C.: National Automobile Dealers Association, 1967.
     Designed as part of a training course to improve automobile dealer merchandising, this text covers in outline business history, early automotive industry history, growth of the auto industry into a giant, and specific ethical rules and practices espoused by the National Automobile Dealers Association.

Nossiter, Bernard D. "The Troubled Conscience of American Business." Harper's 124 (Sept. 1963).

Packard, Vance. The Hidden Persuaders. New York: David McKay, 1957.
     Questions the morality of manipulating consumer tastes and demands through mass motivational techniques.

_____. The Pyramid Climbers. New York: McGraw-Hill, 1962.
     Dramatic observations of the drives of the executive for success within the corporation and the rewards and disappointments to be encountered. Notes and suggested reading list from a modest primer on the corporate executive.

-14-

_____. The Wastemakers. New York: David McKay, 1960.
Another Packard popular expose, this time on the lack of quality,
planned obsolescence and neon commercialization. Seeks to alter
course from artificial stimulation of the economy to a more rational
acceptance of craftsmanship.

Patterson, J. M. "Corporate Behavior and Balance of Power." Business
Horizons 12 (July 1969): 39-52.

Percy, C. H. "Crisis in Public Trust." Michigan Business Review 22
(May 1970): 1-3.

Petit, Thomas A. The Moral Crises in Management. New York:
McGraw-Hill, 1967.

Pike, James A. You and the New Morality:--74 Cases. New York:
Harper & Row, 1967.

"Problems in Ethics." Best's Insurance News 64 (Jan. 1962).

Randall, Clarence Balden. A Creed for Free Enterprise. Boston:
Little, Brown, 1952.

_____. "For a New Code of Business Ethics."
Executive 4 (June 1962).

Randall, John Herman. The Ethical Challenge of a Pluralistic Society.
New York: New York Society for Ethical Culture, 1959.

Robertson, T. "You Have to Pad a Pocket or Two." Electronic News
15 (Mar 9, 1970): 26.

Rosenbaum, E. L. "Are You Happy? or, We Solicit Only Your Surplus
Business." National Underwriters (Life Edition) 29 (Dec. 11, 1965):
2ff.

Ruegg, Fred T. "Ethical Responsibilities of Management." Advanced Management Journal 37 (Feb. 1962).

Savoie, Leonard M. "Business Ethics." Price Waterhouse Review 12 (spring, 1967).

Schein, Edgar H. "The Problem of Moral Education for the Business Manager." Industrial Management Review 6 (fall, 1966): 3-14.

Schuttle, T. F., and L. W. Jacobs. "Business Ethical Dilemma: An Analysis of Conflict." Journal of Purchasing 4 (Nov. 1968): 23-30.

Scott, William A. The Social Ethic in Management Literature. Atlanta: Georgia State College of Business Administration, 1959.

Selekman, Benjamin M. "Cynicism and Managerial Morality." Harvard Business Review 37 (Sept.-Oct. 1958).

_____. A Moral Philosophy for Management. New York: McGraw-Hill, 1959.
    An early insight into the complexities of the business role in social responsibility. The author marks the departure from older attitudes towards a new awareness of corporate influence, noticing that a new framework will be necessary to avoid the confusion normal in change.

_____, and Sylvia K. Selekman. Power and Morality in a Business Society. New York: McGraw-Hill, 1956.
    An astute examination of the definition and uses of power in relationship to moral obligations in public and private arenas.

Shaffer, Charles Louis. "Corporate Membership and Individual Values." Ph.D. dissertation no. 17, 641. New York University, 1956.

Smead, Elmer S. Governmental Promotion and Regulation of Business. New York: Appleton-Century-Crofts, 1969.
     Covers governmental legislation in general, involvement in selected industries and governmental operation of business activities. Includes a number of case examples.

Smith, George Albert, Jr. Business Society and the Individual: Problems in Possible Leadership of Private Enterprise Organizations Operating in a Free Society. Rev. ed. Homewood, Ill.: Richard D. Irwin, 1967.

Sneider, Leopold James. Where Business Fails the Businessman: A Critical Commentary on the Business Establishment. New York: Vantage Press, 1965.

Sorokim, Pitrim A., and Walter A. Lunden. Power and Morality: Who Shall Guard the Guardians? Boston: Porter Sargent, 1959.

Spurrier, William Olivell. Ethics and Business. New York: Scribner, 1962.

Sullivan, A. M. "Business Ethics: Policy or Principle?" Dun's Review and Modern Industry 67 (Nov. 1959).

Sutton, Francis X., et al. The American Business Creed. Cambridge, Mass.: Harvard University Press, 1956.

Sweeney, John F. Danger! Fraud Ahead! Living and Spending Guideposts for the 20th Century American. New York: Exposition Press, 1963.

"Teaching Business Ethics." Dun's Review and Modern Industry 76 (Jan. 1968): 20.

Thompson, Stewart. Management Creeds and Philosophies: Top Management Guides in our Changing Economy. Research Study No. 32. New York: American Management Association, 1958.

Till, Anthony. What You Should Know Before You Buy a Car. Los Angeles: Sherbourne Press, 1968.

"Top Execx Set Company's Moral Tone; NICB Says: Survey Shows Some Companies Issue Ethics Guides; Others are Wary." Advertising Age 35 (Dec. 28, 1964): 16ff.

Towle, Joseph W. Ethics and Standards in American Business. Boston: Houghton Mifflin, 1964.
    A collection of writings on a variety of ethical subjects, this book attempts to focus on professional standards for business management. Five appendices cover existing corporate and industrial codes plus organizations involved in management as a profession.

United Nations. Economic and Social Council. [Ad Hoc Committee on Restrictive Business Practices.] Report to the Economic and Social Council. New York: United Nations, 1953.

_____. Economic and Social Council. Ad Hoc Committee on Restrictive Business Practices. Restrictive Business Practices: Analyses of Governmental Measures Relating to Restrictive Business Practices. New York: United Nations, 1953.

U.S. Business Ethics Advisory Council. A Statement on Business Ethics and a Call for Action. Washington, D.C.: Government Printing Office, 1962.

Van Cise, T. G. "Regulation by Business or Government?" Harvard Business Review 44 (Mar.-Apr. 1966): 53-63.
    Proposes a cooperative effort by business and government to deal with controversial industry trade practices, including case examples and bibliography.

Waddington, C. H. Ethical Animal. London: Allen & Unwin, 1960.

Walton, Clarence C. Ethics and the Executive: Values in Managerial Decision Making. Englewood Cliff, N.J.: Prentice-Hall, 1969.

Watkins, Ralph James. Toward Enlarging the Sphere of Freedom. Berkeley: University of California Press, 1951.

Weisskopf, W., and R. Thain. "Value Research in Business, Economics, Long Overdue." Business and Society 1 (autumn, 1960).

"Whither the Society's Code?" Public Relations Journal 16 (Oct. 1960).

"Who Sets Company's Moral Tone?" Iron Age 111 (Jan. 7, 1965): 129.

"Who Will Watch the Watchman?" National Municipal Review 23 (June 1952): 280.

Williams, Whiting. America's Mainspring and the Great Society. New York: Frederick Fell, 1966.

Wilson, Joseph C. "Social Responsibility of the Businessman." Personnel 48 (Jan.-Feb. 1966).

Winterberger, Henry T. Morality and Business. New Haven: Yale University Press, 1962.

Workshop on Business Ethics. St. Joseph's College. Philadelphia. The Concept of Business Ethics. Ed. Daniel N. DeLucca. Philadelphia: Council on Business Ethics, St. Joseph's College, 1964.

Worthy, James C. Big Business and Free Man. New York: Harper & Brothers, 1959.

-19-

Wraith, A. P. "Growing Concern Shown over Conflict-of-Interest Situations." <u>National</u> <u>Underwriter</u> (Life Edition) 65 (June 3, 1961).

Zech, Robert F. "Ethics in Business: The Responsibility of Management." <u>Financial</u> <u>Executive</u> 32 (July 1963).

Accounting

"Accountants Turn Tougher." Business Week 41 (Oct. 18, 1969): 124-25.

"AICPA Ethics Opinion No. 17: Specialization." New York Certified Public Accountant 36 (Feb. 1966): 155-56.

"American Institute of Accountants. Bylaws--Rules of Professional Conduct. New York: American Institute of Accountants, 1949/50.

American Institute of Certified Public Accountants. Code of Professional Ethics: Numbered Opinions of the Committee on Professional Ethics: Objective of the Institute Adopted by the Council. New York: American Institute of Certified Public Accountants, 1967.
     Code of ethics, opinions, and detailed guidelines for professional practice by accountants.

Barradell, M. Ethics and the Accountant. London: Gee, 1969.

Berg, Kenneth Bernard. Objectivity and Relevance in Accounting Evidence. Ann Arbor, Mich.: University Microfilms, 1953.

Brighton, Gerald David. Social Responsibilities of Public Accountants. Ann Arbor, Mich.: University Microfilms, 1963.

Campfield, William Louis. An Inquiry into the Nature of Judgement Formation and Its Implications to the Public Accounting Profession. Urbana: University of Illinois Press, 1951.

Carey, John L., and William O. Doherty. Ethical Standards of the Accounting Profession. New York: American Institute of Certified Public Accountants, 1966.
     Comprehensive coverage of ethical practices in accounting, ranging in subject matter from public interest to tax practice. Appendices include Code of Ethics and Opinions of American Institute of Certified Public Accountants, although this book is not an official AICPA publication.

Carmichael, D. P., and R. J. Swieringer. "Compatability of Auditing Independence and Management Services--an Identification of Issues." Accounting Review 43 (Oct. 1968): 697-705.

"Conflicts of Interest." Price Waterhouse Review 6 (winter, 1961).

"Ethics--The Unwritten Code." Price Waterhouse Review 8 (spring, 1963).

Lees, Charles R. "Moral Responsibility in Tax Practice." Journal of Accountancy 55 (Apr. 1959).

Leonard, E. C., Jr. "Conscience of Public Accounting." Financial Executive 37 (Apr. 1969): 19ff.

Miller, T. "Professional Responsibility." Journal of Accounting 129 (May 1970): 74-77.

Murray, Edwards B. "Conflicts of Interest." Internal Auditor 19 (fall, 1962).

Price, L. "Review of Professional Conduct Rule #4." New York Certified Public Accountant 35 (July 1965): 314-16.

"Regulation of the Commissioner of Education or the Professional Conduct of Accountants." New York Certified Public Accountant 35 (Oct. 1965): 788-90.

Ring, R. R. "Professional Ethics of the Future." Journal of Accounting 120 (July 1965): 40-41.

Advertising

Books and References

Association of Better Business Bureaus. A Guide for Retail Advertising
and Selling. Comp. and ed. E. W. Gallagher, Kenneth Wood, et al.
5th rev. ed. New York: Association of Better Business Bureau, 1956.
    This book is comprised of a guide and reference to fair-practice
standards and definitions for retail advertising and selling, with a
dictionary index of trade terms, standards, and descriptions.

Bachrach, Arthur J. "The Ethics of Tachistoscopy." Bulletin of the
Atomic Scientists 15 (May 1959): 212-15.
    Bachrach gives a concise nontechnical explanation of subliminal
projection, outlines the arguments in favor of and in opposition to its
use, concluding that the use of subliminal advertising is not in keeping
with accepted ethical standards.

Garrett, Thomas M. An Introduction to Some Ethical Problems of Modern
American Advertising. Rome: Gregorian University Press, 1961.

Hyde, Samuel Y. "Is Advertising Moral?" America 53 (Mar. 11, 1961):
760.

International Chamber of Commerce. International Commission on
Advertising. Advertising Conditions and Regulations in Various
Countries. Rev. ed. Basel: Verlag für Recht und Gesellschaft, 1953.

Mannes, Marya. But Will It Sell? New York: J. B. Lippincott

National Better Business Bureau. Do's and Don'ts in Advertising Copy.
Ed. Allan E. Bockman. New York, National Better Business Bureau.
    A looseleaf service for advertisers, advertising agencies, broad-
casters, and printed media.

Pease, Otis A. The Responsibilities of American Advertising: Private Control and Public Influence, 1920-1940. New Haven: Yale University Press, 1958.

Quinn, Francis X., ed. Ethics, Advertising and Responsibility. Westminster, Md.: Canterbury Press, 1963.

Research Institute of America. Pricing, Selling, Advertising in a Competitive Market. New York: Research Institute of America, 1952.

Simon, Norton T. The Law for Advertising and Marketing. New York: W. W. Norton, 1956.

U.S. Advertising Advisory Commission. Self-Regulation in Advertising. Washington, D.C.: Government Printing Office, 1964.
A report on the operation of private enterprise in an important area of public responsibility, submitted by the Advertising Advisory Commission to the Secretary of Commerce.

Articles and Periodicals

"Advertisers of Travel Contest Arrested in L. A." Advertising Age 40 (May 20, 1969). 3ff.

"Advertising Group Outlines Nine Point Truth Code." Broadcasting 70 (Apr. 11, 1966): 96-97.

"American Brands Ask Injunction vs. TV Guidelines." Advertising Age 40 (Dec. 27, 1969): 1ff.

"American Brands Loses First Round." Broadcasting 77 (Dec. 22, 1969): 26ff.

"American Brands Wages Battle on Two Fronts." Broadcasting 79 (July 13, 1970): 20.

"American Encounters Court Rebuff." Broadcasting 78 (Jan. 5, 1970): 30-31.

"The Bad, the Bare and the Beautiful." Mediascope 13 (Nov. 1969): 35-39.

Bernstein, H. R. "Stick to Claims You Can Prove, Weinberger Advises Businessmen." Advertising Age 41 (May 4, 1970): 1ff.

"Board Seeks Rating in Movie Spots." Broadcasting 76 (May 5, 1969): 40.

"Broadcasters Left With No Cards to Play." Broadcasting 77 (July 28, 1969): 19-22.

"Broadcasters Liable for False Ads?" Broadcasting 75 (Apr. 27, 1970): 49.

"Chevron Ads May Have to Call Its F-310 Ads False." Advertising Age 41 (July 13, 1970): 2.

Christopher, M. "American Won't Alter Pall Mall, Silva Thins Ads; Other Marketers Rush to Meet New Rules." Advertising Age 40 (Dec. 29, 1969): 2ff.

_____. "Excedrin Revises NBC Banned Ad; CBS, ABC Accept Rewritten Version." Advertising Age 41 (Mar. 30, 1970): 5ff.

"Code Authority Minutes Show Trials/Tribulations of Industry Self-Regulation." Advertising Age 40 (July 23, 1969): 106.

"Code of Ethics or Canons of Journalism." Editor and Publisher 102 (Oct. 11, 1959): 9.

"Code Unit Keeps Line Bra Ad Rule, but May Ease It." Advertising Age 40 (Dec. 14, 1969): 2.

Cohen, S. E. "AAF Self-Policing Push Comes Late; Self-Scrutiny by Admen Seen Needed." Advertising Age 41 (July 6, 1970): 52.

_____. "Advertising Claims Come Under Increasingly Piercing Scrutiny." Advertising Age 41 (July 13, 1970): 10.

Cone, F. M. "Disparaging Ads Will Injure All Business; Abuses Can Bring Ban on Competitive Claims." Advertising Age 36 (Sept. 27, 1965): 4ff.

"Consumer Laws Will Change Advertising." Editor and Publisher 103 (Feb. 7, 1970): 15.

"Curtailment of Ads for X Films Spreads." Editor and Publisher 102 (Dec. 6, 1969): 15.

"Dallas Business Leaders Kick off Drive to Implement AFA-AAW Ad Code for Business." Advertising Age 37 (Apr. 18, 1966): 95.

"Decision Made to Switch and Fight." Broadcasting 78 (Jan. 12, 1970): 28.

"Dirty Old Admen Strike Back at Critic." Advertising Age 40 (Dec. 8, 1969): 1ff.

"Effective Self-Discipline of Ad Industry Grows Worldwide: Chamber of Commerce." Advertising Age 41 (May 25, 1970): 111.

"11 Criteria for False Advertising Specified in Bill." Advertising Age 40 (Nov. 24, 1969): 3ff.

"Excedrin Ads Hit in Citizens' Suit Under FTC Law." Advertising Age
41 (July 27, 1970): 1ff.

"Exquisit Form Girds for Girdle Ad Battle w/NAB." Advertising Age 40
(Dec. 8, 1969): 36.

"FCC Backs Across Board Media Treatment on Cigarette Advertising."
Advertising Age 40 (Sept. 22, 1969): 8.

"FCC Issues Warning About Kickbacks." Broadcasting 78 (July 8,
1970): 52.

"FCC Shapes Rule to Halt Plugola." Broadcasting 89 (May 18, 1970):
50.

Finn, David. "Struggle for Ethics in Public Relations." Harvard Business
Review 38 (Jan.-Feb. 1959).

"Four A's Hits Derogatory Ads." Advertising Age 37 (Feb. 21, 1969):
1ff.

"FTC Hits AAMCO on Ad Deception." Advertising Age 41 (July 22,
1970): 69.

"Greenland Bets Admen's Ethics; Ask for Accreditation Setup."
Advertising Age 41 (Feb. 16, 1970): 3.

"Group Is Proposed for Ad Ethics." Broadcasting 78 (Feb. 16, 1970):
33.

"Has NAB Found Cigarette Answer?" Broadcasting 77 (July 14, 1969):
19-21.

"House Okays Bill Aimed at Curbing Sex-slanted Ads." Advertising Age
41 (May 4, 1970): 97.

"Is Nudity Sexy or Just More Honest?" <u>American Druggist</u> 159 (May 19, 1970): 66.

"Judge Fines, Enjoins California Auto Dealer on False Advertising Complaint." <u>Advertising Age</u> 37 (Apr. 11, 1966): 22.

"Judge Reaffirms Dailys Right to Refuse Ads." <u>Advertising Age</u> 40 (Dec. 29, 1969): 4.

"Judge Says Publicity Didn't Harm Pill Case." <u>Editor and Publisher</u> 98 (June 12, 1965): 24.

"Kastor Hilton is Fined $50,000 for Regimen Ad Role." <u>Advertising Age</u> 35 (July 28, 1965): 1ff.

Levitt, T. "Morality (?) of Advertising." <u>Harvard Business Review</u> 48 (July-Aug. 1970): 84-92.

Lucroft, H. "Charges Fly over Balloon Ads for Chevron Gas Additive." <u>Advertising Age</u> 41 (Apr. 6, 1970): 32-33.

"Lying Ads Cause Generation Gap, Freeberg Asserts." <u>Advertising Age</u> 40 (Dec. 8, 1969): 2.

McGannar, D. H. "Advertisers Aid to Broadcasters." <u>Broadcasting</u> 70 (May 2, 1966): 28ff.

"Many Groups Endorse Ad Code." <u>Editor and Publisher</u> 99 (Mar. 19, 1966): 27.

"Mass. Steps Up Fine on Cigarette Bill." <u>Broadcasting</u> 77 (Nov. 17, 1969): 45.

"MBS Affiliates Seek Test of Ad-Ban Law." <u>Broadcasting</u> 78 (May 18, 1970): 28.

"More Smoke on the Cigarette Issue." Broadcasting 77 (Nov. 10, 1969): 27-28.

"Mutual Talks of Court Fight on Cigarette Ad Ban." Advertising Age 41 (July 1, 1970): 8.

"NAB Cigarette Code Faces Court Test." Broadcasting 77 (Dec. 15, 1969): 42.

"NAB Cigarette Code Met Plenty of Resistance, Testimony Reveals." Advertising Age 40 (July 16, 1969): 95.

"NAB Code Rapped by Tobacco Spokesman." Broadcasting 77 (Dec. 8, 1969): 30ff.

"NAB Rejects Ads for a Battery Booster; Agency Defends Them." Advertising Age 41 (Feb. 2, 1970): 68.

"NAB's Interpretation of Tobacco Ad Issue." Broadcasting 77 (Oct. 13, 1969): 25-28.

"National Better Business Bureau Lists Ads Naming Competitors as Insidious; Not So Fast, Says ANA." Advertising Age 36 (Nov. 8, 1965): 1ff.

"NBC Takes Excedrin Ad off Air After Complaint by Sterling Drug." Advertising Age 41 (Mar. 23, 1970): 1ff.

"New Fraudulent Billing Rules Laid Down." Broadcasting 78 (May 25, 1970): 34.

"New Swedish Federation Launches Program Against Misleading Ads." Advertising Age 40 (Sept. 22, 1969): 84.

"9 Categories of Misleading Ads Attached." Editor and Publisher 102 (Aug. 16, 1969): 53.

"No Relaxation on Astrology Ban." Broadcasting 77 (Jan. 12, 1970): 28ff.

"Now Showing--Only Movies Fit for the Family." Editor and Publisher 102 (Nov. 8, 1969): 16.

O'Connor, T. "Shifting Social Scene Presents New Ad Acceptability Problems to Times." Advertising Age 40 (Dec. 22, 1969): 12.

"Options Dwindle for Cigarette Ads on TV." Advertising Age 40 (July 7, 1969): 1ff.

"Promotional Materials Due to Publisher's Motive, Says High Court in Eros Ruling." Advertising Age 37 (Mar. 28, 1966): 4.

"Rekas Forms Group of Better Broadcasting; Argues Admen Lose Ethical Responsibility." Advertising Age 41 (Apr. 20, 1970): 34.

"RKO General Seeks to Join NAB Code." Broadcasting 77 (Dec. 15, 1969): 44.

"Rocky Hits Radio Rejection of Comparative Price Ads; Says Trust Should be Criterion." Advertising Age 40 (May 26, 1969): 32.

"Rule Ads Revamped After Disappointed by NAB Code Board." Advertising Age 40 (July 2, 1969): 113.

Sederberg, K. "Dirty Old Adman Accusation Splits AA Correspondents down the Middle." Advertising Age 40 (Dec. 22, 1969): 3ff.

"Sex Formula Fraud Charge Is Dropped by Post Office; Examiner Cites Inaction by FDS; Marketer Says Fems Relieve Tiredness." Advertising Age 36 (Dec. 13, 1965): 10.

"Sex in Ads Unabated in LA Magazine, Dropped as Too Demure."
Advertising Age 40 (Dec. 15, 1969): 3.

"Sex in Advertising: Are Movie Ads Now in Censor's Focus?" Editor
and Publisher 99 (Mar. 26, 1966): 16.

"Showdown This Week on Cigarettes." Broadcasting 76 (July 16,
1969): 26ff.

"Skeptic Berates NAB Self-regulation." Broadcasting 77 (Dec. 8,
1969): 30.

Stewart, D. C. "Overly Competitive Ads Invite Action by U.S."
Advertising Age 36 (Nov. 15, 1965): 68.

"Study Reveals Ethical Gap; Agency Executives Oppose Some Practices
but Believe Other Admen Don't." Advertising Age 36 (July 5, 1965):
35-36.

"Sucrets Told to End 'Kills Germs' Claim in Its Ads." Advertising Age
36 (May 24, 1965): 2ff.

Sweeney, C. "Advertising Should Know What Product Does, Not What
Client Feels It Does." Advertising Age 36 (Nov. 1, 1965): 1ff.

"Text of Supreme Court Decision on Direct Mail." Advertising Age 41
(May 11, 1970): 92.

"Three Sad Stories from the Concerned Consumer." Advertising Age 41
(Mar. 2, 1970): 56.

"Truth and the Image of Advertising." Journal of Marketing 33
(Oct. 1969): 64-66.

"TV Folk Wary of Sexier Ads, but See 'Em As a Reflection of Times."
Advertising Age 40 (May 26, 1969): 3ff.

"Urges Greater Use of Restraint in Ads." Advertising Age 37 (Jan. 17, 1966): 2.

"Utah Court Case Test Media, Ad Responsibility, Misleading Ads Prepared by Agency for Dealers, Radio, TV Charge Reads." Advertising Age 35 (Dec. 13, 1965): 3ff.

"Vaginal Spray TV Ads Help Drug Store Sales." Journal of American Druggist 159 (May 19, 1969): 52.

"Validity of NAB Code Disputed as Cigarette Ad Bill Moves to House." Advertising Age 40 (July 16, 1969): 1ff.

"War Looms on Radio-TV Obscenity." Broadcasting 77 (Dec. 5, 1969): 58.

"Weinberg Puts Heavy Emphasis on Truthful Ad and Sales Practices." Advertising Age 41 (May 25, 1970): 122.

"What Shoppers Gripe About Most in Their Dealings with Retailers." Merchandise Week 100 (July 22, 1968): 24.

Finance

"Conflict of Interest Crackdown." Business Week 31 (Sept. 24, 1960).
      Results of a United Shareholders' survey.

Cormier, Frank. Wall Street's Shady Side. Introduction by Ferdinand Pecora. Washington, D.C.: Public Affairs Press, 1962.

"Form New Group on Mutual Fund, Insurance Ethics." National Underwriter 73 (Apr. 18, 1969): 35.

Landrum, R. K. "Bankers' Code of Conduct." Bankers Magazine 153 (spring, 1970): 70-73.

McNew, Bennie B., and Charles L. Prather. Fraud Control for Commercial Banks. Homewood, Ill.: Richard D. Irwin, 1962.

Martin, James R. "Ethical Considerations in the Life Insurance Business." Best's Life News 67 (Feb. 1966).

Martin, T. T. R. "Scores 'If We Don't, Someone Else Will'. Business Philosophy." National Underwriter (Life Edition) 69 (Dec. 4, 1965): 2ff.
      Ethics in the life insurance field.

"New Organization for Fund and Insurance Joint Distributors is Formed." Insurance 70 (Apr. 12, 1969): 3ff.

Pratt, Lester A. Bank Frauds, Their Detection and Prevention. New York: Ronald Press, 1965.

Quay, T. G. "Bulls, Bears and Ethics." Management Review 57 (Sept. 1968): 20-24.

Labor and Management

"Code of Ethics." Personnel Administrator 15 (May-June, 1963).

"Code of Ethics for Personnel Administration." Personnel Journal 38 (June 1959).

Collier, Abram T. "Dilemma in Human Relations." Harvard Business Review 33 (Sept.-Oct. 1955).

"Dedication to Others." Personnel Journal 48 (July 1969): 544-45.

Domke, Martin. Commercial Arbitration. New York: Prentice-Hall, 1965.

Dulles, Foster R. Labor in America: A History. New York: Thomas Y. Crowell, 1966.

"Ethics and the Supervisor." Supervisory Management 9 (Nov. 1964).

"Ethics in Personnel Administration." Personnel 34 (Nov. 1953).

Fulmer, Robert M. "Business Ethics: The View from the Campus." Personnel 49 (Mar.-Apr. 1968).

Gorz, Andre. Strategy for Labor. Boston: Beacon Press, 1964.

Habry, B. C. Cases in Labor Relations and Collective Bargaining. New York: Ronald Press, 1966.

Hall, Cameron P., ed. On-the-Job Ethics. New York: National Council of Churches of Christ in the U.S.A., 1963.

Kellogg, Marion S. "The Ethics of Employee Appraisal." Personnel (July-Aug. 1965).

Kennedy, Thomas. Automation Funds and Displaced Workers. Boston: Harvard Business School, 1962.

Labor's Public Responsibility. Madison, Wis.: National Institute of Labor Education, 1960.

Lazarus, Steven, et al. Resolving Business Disputes: The Potential of Commercial Arbitration. New York: American Management Association, 1965.

Lester, Richard Allen. The Economics of Labor. 2nd ed. New York: Mcmillan, 1964.

Lewis, Arthur H. Lament for the Molly Maguires. New York: Harcourt, Brace & World, 1964.

Miller, J. Irwin. The Corporation and the Union. Santa Barbara: Center for the Study of Democratic Institutions, 1962.

National Association of Manufacturers. Moral and Ethical Standards in Labor and Management; Abstracted from the Code of Ethics, Credo and Official Policies of the National Association of Manufacturers--The Ethical Practices Code of the American Federation of Labor and Congress of Industrial Organizations. New York: National Association of Manufacturers, 1958.

Okum, Arthur M., ed. The Battle Against Unemployment. New York: W. W. Norton, 1965.

Russon, Allien R. Business Behavior. 3rd ed. Cincinnati: South-Western Publishing Co., 1964.

Safire, W. L. "Spy Who Went Out in the Heat: A Story of Business Ethics." Public Relations Journal 22 (Feb. 1966): 14-18.

Spates, Thomas G. _Human Values Where People Work_. New York: Harper & Row, 1960.

"Stealing Employees is Bad Business." _Iron Age_ 202 (July 4, 1968): 25.

Symposium on Ethics, 3d, University of Minnesota, 1967. _Ethics and Employment_. Minneapolis, Minn.: University of Minnesota, 1960.
  Lectures by Eli Ginzberg, George W. England, Roger Wheeler.

Viorst, Milton, and J. V. Reistrup. "Radon Daughters and the Federal Government." _Bulletin of The Atomic Scientists._ 23 (Oct. 1967): 25-29.
  Points out failure of the federal government to provide adequate working safety conditions for uranium miners exposed to radiation as a result of management and congressional pressure.

Whyte, William H., Jr. _Is Anybody Listening?_ New York: Simon & Schuster, 1952.

_____. _The Organization Man._ Garden City, N.Y.: Doubleday Anchor Books, 1956.

Marketing

American Management Association. Trade Relations Defined: The
Concept, Legal Aspects, Ethical Problems. New York: American
Management Association, 1962.

Bartels, Robert. "A Model for Ethics in Marketing." Journal of Marketing 31 (Jan. 1967): 20-26.

"Chrysler Adopts Rules on Vendors." New York Times (Feb. 2, 1961).

Classen, Earl A. "Marketing Ethics and the Consumer." Harvard
Business Review 45 (Jan.-Feb. 1967): 79-86.

Glasser, Ralph. The New High Priesthood: The Social, Ethical and
Political Implications of a Marketing Oriented Society. London:
Macmillan, 1967.

"Identical Price Bids: Often Legal, but Definitely Taboo." Sales
Management 43 (May 5, 1961).

Magnuson, Warren G. The Dark Side of the Marketplace. Englewood
Cliffs, N.J.: Prentice-Hall, 1968.
    A U.S. senator's investigation of deceptive and fraudulant
business practices, it contains a brief but useful bibliography.

"Oh, the Sexy Things They're Saying About Montgomery Ward!" Sales
Management 104 (May 15, 1970): 26-27.

Oppenheim, Saul Chesterfield. Unfair Trade Practices: Cases and
Comments. 2nd ed. St. Paul, Minn.: West Publishing Co., 1965.

Patterson, James M. "What Are the Social and Ethical Responsibilities
of Marketing Executives?" Journal of Marketing 30 (July 1966):
12-15.

Prester, Lee E. _Social Issues in Marketing: Readings for Analysis._
Glenview, Ill.: Scott, Foresman, 1968.

Rostow, Eugene V. "The Ethics of Competition Revisited." _California
Management Review_ 5 (spring, 1963).

"Salesmanship and Professional Standards." _Agent and Representative_
12 (Dec. 1961).

Twedt, Dick Warren. "Why a Marketing Research Code of Ethics?"
Journal of Marketing 27 (Oct. 1963).

Production

"Code of Ethics Recommended: Statement of Recommended Ethical Conduct for the Construction Industry." Electrical Construction and Maintenance 57 (Nov. 1959): 227-29.

"Ethics of Planned Obsolescence." Machine Design 36 (Aug. 27, 1964): 136-38.

Forbert, O. M. "Code of Ethics of Master Printers of New Zealand." Graphic Arts 41 (Nov. 1969): 95.

Grund, C. B. "Ethics of the Total Environmental System." Heating, Piping, and Air-Conditioning 38 (Dec. 1966): 113-16.
    This detailed report stresses the consulting engineer's need for ethics in providing his client with full and objective information and fair recommendations.

Holloway, Robert J. "Research on Purchasing Ethics." Journal of Purchasing 1 (Nov. 1965).

Michael, Donald H. Cybernation: The Silent Conquest. Santa Barbara, Calif.: Center for the Study of Democratic Institutions, 1962.

Mumford, Lewis. The Myth of the Machine. New York: Harcourt, Brace & World, 1966.

Nader, Ralph. Unsafe at Any Speed. New York: Grossman, 1965.
    Classic attack on Detroit and the quality and safety of American automobiles.

Ryan, Brother Leo V. "Business Ethics and Purchasing." Journal of Purchasing 2 (Nov. 1966).

Simon, Herbert A. The Shape of Automation for Man and Management. New York: Harper & Row, 1965.

Religion and Business

Birkly, Luther John. Contemporary Ethical Theories. New York: Philosophical Library, 1961.

Bursk, Edward Collins, ed. Business and Religion: A New Depth Dimension in Management. New York: Harper & Brothers, 1959.

Clark, John Wilham. Religion and the Moral Standard of American Businessman. Cincinnati: South-Western Publishing Co., 1966.

Conference on Business and the Social Order, Valparaiso University. The Christian in Business: Thoughts on Business and the Social Order. Ed. Andrew J. Buehner. St. Louis, Mo.: Lutheran Academy for Scholarship, 1966.

Eisenstadt, Shmuel Noah, comp. The Protestant Ethic and Modernization: A Comparative View. New York: Basic Books, 1968.

Fanfani, Amintore. Catholicism, Protestantism and Capitalism. New York: Sheed & Ward, 1955.

Guiseppe, B. M., J. De Senarclens, and J. J. Groen. "Human Experimentation--A World Problem from the Standpoint of Spiritual Leaders." (symposium). World Medical Journal 7 (May 1960): 80-83, 96.

Hassett, J. D. "Freedom and Order Before God: A Catholic View." New York University Law Review 31 (1956): 1170-88.

Hospers, John. Human Conduct: An Introduction to the Problems of Ethics. New York: Harcourt, Brace & World, 1961.

Institute for Religious and Social Studies, Jewish Theological Seminary of America. Conflict of Loyalties. Ed. R. M. MacIver. New York: Harper & Row, 1969.

-40-

_____. Patterns of Ethics in America Today. Ed. F.
Ernest Johnson. New York: Harper & Brothers, 1960.

Mitchell, John E. The Christian in Business. Westwood, N.J.: Fleming
H. Revell, 1967.

Murran, George. There Is a Place for God in Business: Spiritual Guide
for Business. New York: Pageant Press, 1956.

National Conference of Christians and Jews. Religious Freedom and
Public Affairs Project. Religious Responsibility for the Social Order,
a Symposium by Three Theologians: Jaroslav Pelikan, Gustavo Wiegel
and Emil L. Fackenheim. New York: National Conference of Christians
and Jews, 1962.

Natural Law & Christian Ethics, the Contemporary Catholic Vice of the
Moral Order. Ed. Graham Moffatt Jamieson, Ph.D. New York:
Columbia University Press, 1951.

Northcott, Clarence Hunter. Christian Principles in Industry and Their
Application in Practice. London: Pitman, 1958.

Obenhaus, Victor. Ethics for an Industrial Age: A Christian Inquiry.
Edited, with an afterword, by F. Ernest Johnson. New York: Harper
& Brothers, 1965.

Regan, Richard T. American Pluralism and the Catholic Conscience.
With a forword by John Courtney Murray. New York: Macmillan,
1963.

Smart, John Jamieson Carswell. An Outline of a System of Utilitarian
Ethics. Carlton, Australia: Melbourne University Press, 1961.

Worthy, James C. "Religion and Its Role in the World of Business."
Journal of Business 30 (Oct. 1958).

ENGINEERING

References and Books

Alger, Philip L., N. A. Christensen, and Sterling P. Olmsted. Ethical
Problems in Engineering. Ed. Barrington S. Hanson and John A. Miller.
New York: Wiley, 1965.

Association of Consulting Management Engineers. Standards of Professional Conduct and Practice. New York: Association of Consulting
Management Engineers, 1963.

Danielson, Lee E. Characteristics of Engineers and Scientists. Ann
Arbor, Mich.: University of Michigan Press, 1960.
    Managerial policies and practices conducive to improved per-
formance of engineers and scientists.

Mantell, Murray I. Ethics and Professionalism in Engineering. New
York: Macmillan, 1964.

Articles and Codes

"AIA Clarifies Its Ethical Standards." Engineering News Record 173
(July 30, 1964): 12.

"AIA to Clarify Employment Ethics." Engineering News Record 173
(July 16, 1964): 23.

Abernathy, James M. "Some Ethical Implications of Professional
Planning." American Society of Civil Engineers, Journal of Professional Practice. 90 (May 1964): 23-29.
    The author contends that the movement to establish planning as
a profession carries ominous ethical implications; he argues that it is
the responsibility of the engineering profession to see that planning
reoccupies its proper place as an integral part of the total engineering
operation.

_____. "Some Ethical Implications of Professional Planning."
American Society of Civil Engineers, Journal of Professional Practice 91
(Sept. 1965): 86-89.
    This extends the author's original argument concerning the
necessity for integration of the planning function into the total engineering operation.

Alderman, Frank E. "Ethics and Municipal Engineers in Private Practice."
American Society of Civil Engineers Journal of Professional Activities
92 (May 1966): 67-68.

Alexander, R. L. "How to Publish and Perish." Civil Engineering 37
(June 1967): 77-78.
    Supports participation of engineers and designers in the processes
of political decision-making, rather than remaining mere mechanics.

Anonymous Management Consultant. "Gathering Competitive Intelligence." Chemical Engineering 73 (Apr. 25, 1966): 143-48.
    The ethical questions raised in this article concern involvement
of engineers and other scientists in methods of obtaining competitive
data and information.

"Architects Move to Enforce New Ethics." Engineering News Record 174
(Jan. 7, 1965): 22-23.

"Architects Toughen Ethical Standards." Engineering News Record 172
(June 25, 1964): 17-18.

Becker, W. C. "More on Ethics: Protection for the Employer."
Chemical Engineering Progress 61 (Apr. 1965): 33-35.
    This article argues for the employer's right to maintain trade
secrets and classified information from transfer outside the organization by employees.

Beer, Charles G. "Some Ethical Implications of Professional Planning."
American Society of Civil Engineers, Journal of Professional Practice 91
(Jan. 1965): 59-60.
    An extension of the debate over the role of the planning function
in engineering.

Biedermann, H. G. "Ethics in Negotiating with Prospective Employers." Proceedings of the American Society of Chemical Engineers 93 (Dec. 1967): 27-31.

"Canons of Ethics for Engineering." ASHRAE Journal 4 (Oct. 1962): 18.

Charyk, J. V. "Scientist and His Responsibility." Aerospace Engineering 20 (July 7, 1961): 7.
    In this piece, the engineer as scientist is held responsible to society for ethical and social behavior.

Christensen, N. A. "Function of Ethical Codes." Petroleum Management 37 (Oct. 1965): 72-75.
    Maintains that engineers require a professional code of ethics that fits the unique characteristics of different engineering technologies. Includes examples of ethical codes and situations.

_____. "Purpose of Professional Engineering Ethics." Mechanical Engineering 87 (Nov. 1965): 46-48.
    The author considers five professional engineering societies and lists codes and particular types of ethical problems peculiar to each.

Cisler, W. L. "Engineer in International Affairs." Mechanical Engineering 82 (Feb. 1960): 54-56.
    The role of the professional engineer in matters of foreign policy.

Clyde, G. D. "Engineer and Politics." Civil Engineering 30 (Aug. 1960): 45-46.
    The role of the professional engineer in public planning and decision-making.

"Code of Ethics." Consulting Engineer 14 (Apr. 1964).

Code of Ethics." Naval Engineers Journal 77 (Feb. 1965): 45-47.
    Reports the approved new code of ethics for engineers as promulgated by the National Society of Professional Engineers.

-44-

"Code of Ethics as Amended to Be Voted On by ASCE Membership."
Civil Engineering 31 (June 1961): 42-44.
    The Code of Ethics of the American Society of Civil Engineers,
proposed amendments, and the ASCE's "Guide to Professional Practice
Under the Code of Ethics."

Cohen, Edward. "Criticism and the Advancement of Building Engineering." Civil Engineering 37 (July 1967): 34-35.
    Critical evaluation of engineers' professional public performance
is seen as an obligation of both individual engineers and the profession
as a whole.

"Conflicts of Interest Pose No Big Problem." Chemical and Engineering
News 38 (Oct. 23, 1961).

Cutler, C. D. "Duty to Dissent." IEEE Spectrum 4 (June 1967): 47.

Davis, A. S. "Ethics and the Engineer, and What the Law Has to Say
About Both of Them." Product Engineering 36 (July 5, 1965): 70-75.
    Based on a lecture to the New York State Society of Professional
Engineers, this discussion covers ethical ramifications of job mobility,
industrial intelligence and scientific creativity.

Dinsmore, R. P. "It's the Individual's Responsibility." Chemical
Engineering Progress 61 (Apr. 1965): 38.
    One responsibility of the professional engineer is awareness
of ethical issues and standards, as well as adherence to standards
as established by the profession.

"Engineers Speak out on Ethics." Chemical Engineering 70 (Dec. 9,
1963): 177-84.
    Considers the results of a poll on ethical codes, with interpreta-
tion of the data acquired.

"Ethical Problems in Engineering." Petroleum Management 37 (Oct.
1965): 76-77.
    Two case situations and analyses involving ethical behavior of
engineers are the focus of this brief discussion.

"Ethics in Business." Chemical Engineering Progress 61 (Feb. 1965): 13-25.

    This article separates business aspects of chemical engineering from scientific functions on the subject of ethical behavior.

Gray, A. W. "When an Engineer Leaves a Company, What Are the Rights and Obligations of Employee and Employer?" Machine Design 65 (Mar. 28, 1963): 133-34.

    Another article on the ethical and legal problems of engineers in job-switching and competitive information.

Gray, H. "Obligations of Engineers." Plant Engineering 17 (Feb. 1963): 155.

    Discourse on the ethical and social responsibilities of the professional engineer.

"How Useful Are Our Ethical Codes?" Chemical Engineering 70 (Sept. 2, 1963): 87-90.

    An attempt to gather response on ten ethical situations as the basis for formulating potential codes of behavior.

"In Public Affairs Has Science Been Overemphasized to the Detriment of Engineering?" Product Engineering 31 (Mar. 14, 1960): 24-25.

    Science has received governmental emphasis to the detriment of engineering, from a public standpoint.

"Interpretation of the ASCE Code of Ethics." Civil Engineering 30 (Jan. 1960): 25-27.

    Official interpretation of the American Society of Civil Engineers' code of ethics is given by the Board of Direction of the ASCE.

Jolly, J. B. "Needed: Stronger Engineering Groups." Chemical Engineering 71 (Aug. 3, 1964): 112-16.

    Comparison of engineering with medicine as a profession, with the argument that the inclusion of nonprofessionals in engineering has precluded formulation of an effective set of ethical codes and standards.

Krause, Axel. "Trade Secrets: Robert Aries Airs His Views." Chemical Engineering 73 (Apr. 11, 1966): 175-78.
    Interview with Robert S. Aries outlines ethical and legal implications of handling of competitive information.

Labine, R. A. "Engineers Ask for Action." Chemical Engineering 72 (Feb. 15, 1965): 188ff.
    Report on professional activism by engineers, indicating support for an ethical review board.

_____. "Where Is Engineering Pointing." Chemical Engineering 71 (Oct. 26, 1964): 138ff.
    Points attention to the engineering profession's need for a clearinghouse for ethical problems and situations.

Lee, Louis. "The Younger Viewpoint--Social Consciousness." Civil Engineering 37 (Feb. 1967): 71.
    Greater breadth in the education of engineers and more community-level involvement are espoused as a means of fulfilling public responsibilities.

Lessels, G. A. "Stepping-Stones to Professionalism." Chemical Engineering 71 (Aug. 31, 1964): 86-90.
    An argument for increased levels of awareness of ethical behavior and standards as the basis for true professionalism.

McNamara, Raymond W. "The Younger Viewpoint--Code of Ethics." Civil Engineering 37 (Feb. 1967): 71.
    Describes the role of a professional organization, the American Society of Civil Engineers, in enforcement and maintenance of its code of ethics.

Marlowe, D. E. "Legacy of Merlin." Mechanical Engineering 86 (Feb. 1, 1964): 26-69.
    The involvement of engineers in governmental decision-making is likened to Merlin's advisory position to King Arthur, underlining the need for more positive action.

"Measuring Engineering Efficiency." Chemical Engineering 69 (Dec. 24, 1962): 91-92.
Critics of PACE, a performance and cost evaluation system to measure engineering efficiency, decry use of the method as a form of "old-fashioned spying."

Merris, D. K. "Is the Man Who Designs Responsible to Society?" Product Engineering 38 (Dec. 4, 1967): 116-22.

Minker, R. L. "Another Look at Engineering Ethics." Chemical Engineering 74 (Oct. 9, 1967): 258ff.

"Needed: Ecumenical Ethics: Talks at ASCE's Detroit Meeting." Engineering News Record 169 (Oct. 18, 1962): 22-23.

Nicholson, E. K., and John Gammell. "Ethics and the Technical Societies." Electrical Engineering 81 (Apr. 1962): 260-61.
The authors list procedures for the reviewing and updating of codes of ethics by professional engineering societies.

"NSPE Irked by AIA Ethical Standard." Engineering News Record 173 (July 9, 1964): 29.

Pandullo, Francis. "Ethics and Municipal Engineers in Private Practice." American Society of Civil Engineers Journal of Professional Practice. 91 (Sept. 1965): 1-6.
Discussion of four private practice situations that have potential ethical implications and problems.

Park, I. R. "Are Engineers Too Good for Politics." Product Engineering 31 (Nov. 7, 1960): 24-25.
Various approaches to the role of the engineer in politics and political activities.

"Revised and Expanded Code of Ethics Put to Members: ASCE Meeting, Phoenix, Arizona." Engineering News Record 166 (Apr. 20, 1961): 25-26.

Rowe, R. R. "Ethics in Public Practice." Civil Engineering 29
(Jan. 1959): 1-2.
    Article-by-article discussion of the applicability of the code
of ethics of the American Society of Civil Engineers to the engineer
in private practice.

Rowley, Louis N. "In the Public Interest." Mechanical Engineering
90 (Aug. 1967): 14-16.
    The author, president of the American Society of Mechanical
Engineers, argues that it is the professional duty of the engineer to
assume a role in national planning.

Russell, J. E. "Proper Use of Common Sense and Engineering in
Secondary Recovery." Journal of Petroleum Technology 16 (Sept.
1964): 1003-5.
    The author stresses the need for a formal ethic in the engineer-
ing profession as a basis for uplifting the image of the engineer.

Rzasa, M. J. "Ethics Is a Personal Thing." Chemical Engineering
Progress 61 (Apr. 1965): 35-37.
    The author holds that a code of ethics is necessary for engineer-
ing to be considered a profession. In addition, he recommends, for
engineering students, a course in engineering professionalism, to
include ethics; reference, within the technical curriculum, to ethical
practices; and professional and student seminars on engineering
ethics.

Schuster, R. "Profile of a Real Professional." Plant Engineering 21
(Apr. 1967): 127-30.

Tangerman, E. J. "How Secure Can You Keep Your Design Secrets?"
Product Engineering 37 (July 4, 1966): 87-95.
    Distinction between ethical and unethical practices concerning
design secrets in industry.

Thring, M. W. "Social Responsibility of the Engineer." Electronics
and Power 13 (Aug. 1967): 292-94.

Turner, E. M. "Human Side of Engineering." IEEE Spectrum 4
(July 1967): 70-71.

"What the Code of Ethics Says." Chemical Engineering Progress 61
(Feb. 1965): 39.
    The official code of ethics for chemical engineers is reprinted
here.

Wisely, W. H. "Administration of Ethical Standards." Civil Engineering 37 (Aug. 1967): 37.
    He charges that the American Society of Civil Engineers is
"lackadaisical or ineffective or too lenient in the administration of
the Code of Ethics." The author claims no other engineering society
in the world can match its record in the development and maintenance
of ethical standards. He then presents a summary of professional
conduct cases.

_____. "Product Endorsement by Engineering." Civil
Engineering 35 (Apr. 1965): 41.
    He charges that the American Society of Civil Engineers dis-
cusses details and technicalities of the ethical admonition against
personal testimonial advertisements by engineers.

_____. "Spirit of Service." Civil Engineering 37 (Dec. 31,
1967): 33.
    The author, secretary of tne ASCE, says a profession is char-
acgerized and defined by the ethical spirit of service found within it.

Woohiser, David A., and L. M. Falkson. "Some Ethical Implications
of Professional Planning." American Society of Civil Engineers, Journal
of Professional Practice 91 (Jan. 1965): 58-59.
    Concerns the debate over professional planning as a part of
engineering as a profession.

Wright, P. M. "Worlds of Two Giants." Proceedings of the American
Society of Civil Engineers 92 (Dec. 1966): 1-5.
    The author emphasizes the importance of engineering ethics in
construction and public relations of a contracting firm in addition to
ethics in engineering design.

GENERAL ETHICAL PHILOSOPHY

Bibliographies and References

Johnson, Oliver A., ed. Ethics, A Source Book. New York: Dryden Press, 1958.

Kresge, Elijah Everett. The Search for a Way of Life: A Review of the Major Classical and Contemporary Ethical Systems of the Western World. New York: Exposition Press, 1950.

Selekman, Benjamin Morris. Power and Morality. Cambridge, Mass.: Baker Library, Harvard University, 1963.
    A list of books selected by B. M. Selekman for the Baker Library, Graduate School of Business Administration, Harvard University.

Sinha, Jadunath. A Manual of Ethics. 7th ed., rev. and enl. Calcutta: Sinha Publications House, 1962.

Philosophies, Discourses, and Collected Readings

Adler, Mortimer Jerome. The Time for Our Lives: the Ethics of Common Sense. New York: Holt, Rinehart & Winston, 1970.

Aiken, Henry David. Reason and Conduct: New Bearings in Moral Philosophy. New York: Knopf, 1967.

_____. Ethics and Society: Original Essays on Contemporary Moral Problems. Richard T. DeGeorge. London and Melbourne: Macmillan, 1968.

Angell, Robert Cooley. Free Society & Moral Crisis. Foreword by Reinhold Niebuhr. Ann Arbor: University of Michigan Press, 1958.

Augustin, Leroy George. Come, Let Us Play God. New York: Harper & Row, 1969.

Baylis, Charles Augustis. Ethics, the Principles of Wise Choice. New York: Holt, Rinehart & Winston, 1958.

Beardsmore, R. W. Moral Reasoning. London: Routledge & Kegan Paul, 1969.

Binkley, Luther John. Conflict of Ideas: Changing Values in Western Society. New York: Van Nostrand, 1969.
    Contains bibliography.

Blanshard, Brand. The Impasse in Ethics, and a Way Out. Berkeley: University of California Press, 1955.

Bradley, Francis Herbert. Ethical Studies: Selected Essays. Introduction by Ralph G. Ross. New York: Liberal Arts Press, 1951.

Brody, Boruch A., comp. Moral Rules and Particular Circumstances. Englewood Cliffs, N.J.: Prentice-Hall, 1970.

Coggle, Bertrand J., and John P. K. Byrnes. Christian Social Ethics. Foreword by Edward Rogers. London: Epworth Press, 1956.

Cohen, Laurence Jonathan. The Principles of World Citizenship. Oxford: Blackwell, 1954.

Cook, Fred J. The Corrupted Land: The Social Morality of Modern America. New York: Macmillan, 1966.

David, William Edward. A Comparative Study of the Social Ethics of Walter Rauschenbusch and Reinhold Niebuhr. Ann Arbor, Mich.: University Microfilms, 1959.

Devlin, Sir Patrick. The Enforcement of Morals. London: British Academy, 1959.

Douglas, Paul Howard. In Our Time. New York: Harcourt, Brace & World, 1968.

Ethical Issues in American Life. Ed. Harold W. Fildey. Nashville: Vanderbilt University Press, 1967.
    A seminar sponsored by the divinity school of Vanderbilt University and the Southern Regional Education Board. August 27-September 1, 1967.

Ewing, Alfred Cyril. Ethics. London: English Universities Press, 1953.

Fagothey, Austin. Right and Reason: Ethics in Theory and Practice. St. Louis, Mo.: C. V. Mosby, 1953.

Fischer, Nathan Joseph [Robert Laurence]. Not with Bombs but with an Idea: The Principles of Ethicalism, Gateway to a Democratic Economy at Home and Abroad. New York: Greenwich, 1957.

Garnett, Arthur Campbell. Can Ideals and Norms Be Justified? Stockton, Calif.: College of the Pacific, 1955.

Gauthier, David P., comp. Morality and Rational Self-Interest. Englewood Cliffs, N.J.: Prentice-Hall, 1970.

Girvetz, Harry K., ed. Contemporary Moral Issues. Belmont, Calif.: Wadsworth, 1963.

Goodman, Walter. All Honorable Men: Corruption and Compromise in American Life. Boston: Little, Brown, 1963.

-53-

Gottlieb, Gidon. The Logic of Choice: An Investigation of the Concepts of Rule and Rationality. London: Allen & Unwin, 1968.

Green, Lucile Wolfe. Ethics in the "New Key." Ann Arbor, Mich.: University Microfilms, 1958.

Greet, Kenneth L. The Art of Moral Judgment. London: Epworth, 1970.

Heard, Gerold. Morals Since 1900. London: A. Dahers, 1950.

Hill, Thomas English. Ethics in Theory and Practice. New York: Thomas Y. Crowell, 1956.

Hilliard, Charles Craig. Supremacy and Peace. New York: North River Press, 1956.

International Press Institute. Research Service. Press Councils and Press Codes. 4th ed. Zurich: International Press Institute, 1966.
    A summary prepared by the IPI research service on the basis of texts published in IPI report and other documents.

Jackson, Douglas MacGilchrist. Human Life and Human Worth. London: Christian Medical Fellowship, 1968.

Kattsoff, L. O. Making Moral Decisions. New York: James H. Heineman, 1968.

Kurtz, Paul W. Decision and the Condition of Man. Seattle: University of Washington Press, 1965.

Mayer, Charles Leopold. In Quest of New Ethics. Translated and with a preface by Harold A. Lorrabee. Boston: Beacon Press, 1954.

Mayer, Frederick, and Floyd H. Ross. Ethics and the Modern World: Towards a One World Perspective. Dubuque, Iowa: William C. Brown Co., 1952.

McGlynn, James V., and Jules J. Tover. Modern Ethical Theories. Milwaukee: Bruce Publishing Company, 1962.

Melden, Abraham Irving. Rights and Right Conduct. Oxford: Blackwell, 1959.

Meulder, Walter George. Foundations of the Responsible Society. Nashville: Abington Press, 1959.

Milius, William B. We Are Not Sure of Sorrow. New York: Vantage Press, 1964.

Moore, Thomas Verner. Principles of Ethics. 5th ed. Completely revised by Gregory Stevens. Philadelphia: Lippincott, 1959.

Market, Gordon F. Harvest of the Bitter Seed. Philadelphia: Dorrance, 1959.

Muirhead, John Henry. Rule and End in Morals. Freeport, N.Y.: Books for Libraries Press, 1969.

Oyen, Hendrik Van. Affluence and the Christian. Trans. Frank Clarke. Philadelphia: Fortress Press, 1966.

Parry, Sir Edward Abbott. The Seven Lamps of Advocacy. Freeport, N.Y.: Books for Libraries Press, 1968.

Perla, Leo. Can We End the Cold War? A Study in American Foreign Policy. With a prefatory note by James T. Shotwell. New York: Macmillan, 1960.

Pike, James A. You and the New Morality: 74 Cases. New York: Harper & Row, 1967.

Piper, Otto A. The Christian Meaning of Money. Englewood Cliffs, N.J.: Prentice-Hall, 1965.

Prior, Kenneth Francis William. God and Mammon: The Christian Mastery of Money. Philadelphia: Westminster Press, 1965.

Rader, Melvin Miller. Ethics and the Human Community. New York: Holt, Rinehart & Winston, 1964.

Rotary International. Service Is My Business. Chicago: Rotary International, 1950.

Russell, Bertrand. Sceptical Essays. London: Allen & Unwin; New York: Barnes and Noble, 1961.

Schneider, Herbert Wallace. Three Dimensions of Public Morality. Bloomington: Indiana University Press, 1956.

Selekman, Sylvia (Kipald), and Benjamin M. Selekman. Power and Morality in a Business Society. New York: McGraw-Hill, 1956.

Selram, Howard. Ethics and Progress: New Values in a Revolutionary World. New York: International Publishers, 1965.

Seton Hall University. School of Law. Conference on Professional Responsibility. Newark, N.J.: Seton Hall University, 1956.

Smith, Thomas Vernon, and William Dobbins. Constructive Ethics. Englewood Cliffs, N.J.: Prentice-Hall, 1961.

Sorokim, Pitrim Aleksandrovich, and Walter A. Lunden. Power and Morality: Who Shall Guard the Guardian? Boston: Porter Sargent, 1959.

Spindle, Robert B. _A Surplus of Riches: The Pursuit of Happiness in a Time of Troubles_. Philadelphia: Dorrance, 1968.

Stevens, Edward. _Making Moral Decisions_. Glen Rock, N.J.: Paulist Press, 1969.

Titus, Harold Hopper. _Ethics for Today_. 3rd ed. New York: American Book Co., 1957.

GOVERNMENT

Bibliographies and References

U.S. Library of Congress. Legislative Reference Service. Economic Division. Government and Business: A Selected Bibliography. Washington, D.C.: Library of Congress, 1970.

_____. Legislative Reference Service. Government and General Research Division. Congress and Ethics: Conflict of Interest and Other Dilemmas: A Bibliography. Washington, D.C.: Library of Congress, 1966.

_____. Legislative Reference Service. Government and General Research Division. Congressional Ethics and the Ethics Committees: A Select Annotated Bibliography. Washington, D.C.: Library of Congress, 1970.

_____. Legislative Reference Service. Government and General Research Division. The House Committee on Standards of Official Conduct. Washington, D.C.: Library of Congress, 1968.
    A compendium of this committee's history, findings, and report.

Federal Government

Appleby, Paul H. Morality and Administration in American Government. Baton Rouge: Louisiana State University Press, 1952.

The Association of the Bar of the City of New York. Conflict of Interest and Federal Service. Cambridge, Mass.: Harvard University Press, 1960.

Bailey, Stephen Kemp. "Ethics and the Public Service." Public Administration Review, 24 (Dec. 1964): 234-43.

-58-

Beals, Ralph L. "Cross-Cultural Research and Government Policy."
Bulletin of the Atomic Scientists 23 (Oct. 1967): 18-24.
    Concerned with the effect of government sponsorship (e.g.,
Department of Defense) and government subversion (e.g., CIA) in
anthropological tests and studies.

Bolles, Blair. How to Get Rich in Washington, Rich Man's Division
of the Welfare State. New York: W. W. Norton, 1952.

Buchanan, Scott. The Corporation and the Republic. New York: Fund
for the Republic, 1958.

"Deceptive Ads Under Scrutiny by Senate Unit." Advertising Age 36
(Sept. 20, 1965): 17.

Douglas, Paul Howard. Ethics in Government. Cambridge, Mass.:
Harvard University Press, 1957.
    Commentary on moral standards and problems in government
and recommendations for improvement.

Ethical Standards in Government. Report of a subcommittee of the
Committee on Labor and Public Welfare, United States Senate.
Washington, D.C.: Government Printing Office, 1951.

Hanson, Galen. Candles in Conscience: Ventures in the Statecraft
of Rigor and Restraint. Detroit: Harlo Press, 1965.

Hartley, H. "Science and Government." Chemistry and Industry 80
(Sept. 16, 1961): 1478-80.
    Discussion of the scientific community's role in planning
public policy.

Johnson, George. The Washington Waste Makers. Darby, Conn.:
Monarch Books, 1963.

Kefauver, Estes. In a Few Hands. New York: Pantheon Books, 1965.

Lasagna, L. "Profession, Government and Drug Industry." Lancet 1 (1962): 580-81.

Lear, J. "Drugmakers and the Government--Who Makes the Decisions?" Saturday Review 36 (June 4, 1960): 37-42.

Lilienthal, David E. TVA: Democracy on the March. Chicago: Quandrangle Books, 1966.

Low, George E. "The Camelot Affair." Bulletin of the Atomic Scientists 22 (May 1966): 44-48.
       History of Project Camelot and involvement of various governmental agencies with implications for social science research.

Lumbard, Eliott H. Encouraging Integrity in Office. New York: Citizens Union Research Foundation, 1964.

Margolis, H. "Science Advisory Committee and National Goals Reports Emphasize Growing Roles of Government." Science 132 (Dec. 2, 1960): 1648-49.
       Increasing interaction between science and government.

Minnesota Governor's Commission on Ethics in Government. Ethics in Government. A Report to Governor Orville L. Freeman. St. Paul, Minn.: Minnesota Governor's Commission on Ethics in Government, 1959.

Moneypenny, Phillip. "A Code of Ethics as a Means of Controlling Administrative Conduct." Public Administration Review 13 (summer, 1953).

Sjoberg, Gideon, ed. Ethics, Politics, and Social Research. Cambridge, Mass.: Schenkman Publishing Co., 1967.
       Controversial compendium of essays on ethical and political pressures on social science researchers.

U.S. Congress. House. Subcommittee on Government Operations. Special Inquiry on Invasion of Privacy. Washington, D.C.: Government Printing Office, 1966.

   Contains the hearings before a subcommittee on the House Committee on Government Operations and contains testimony of all witnesses before the committee.

_____. Subcommittee on International Organizations and Movements. Report No. 4 on Winning the Cold War: The U.S. Ideological Offensive. Washington, D.C.: Government Printing Office, 1966.

   Deals with the relationships between the behavioral sciences and the national security.

_____. Senate. Committee on Labor and Public Welfare. Commission on Ethics in Government. Report to Accompany Senate Joint Resolution 107. Washington, D.C.: Government Printing Office, 1951.

_____. Senate. Committee on Labor and Public Welfare. Establishment of a Commission on Ethics in Government. Hearings Before a Subcommittee to Study Senate. Concurrent Resolution 21 of the Committee on Labor and Public Welfare, U.S. Senate, 82nd Congress, first session. Washington, D.C.: Government Printing Office, 1951.

_____. Senate. Committee on Labor and Public Welfare. Ethical Standards in Government. Report of a Subcommittee of the Committee on Labor and Public Welfare, U.S. Senate. Washington, D.C.: Government Printing Office, 1951.

   Proposals for improvement of ethical standards in the federal government including establishment of a commission on ethics in government.

_____. Senate. Committee on Government Operations. Subcommittee on Reorganization in International Organizations. Numerous Studies of "Coordination of Federal Agencies' Programs in Biomedical Research and in Other Scientific Areas," "Interagency Coordination in Drug Research and Regulation," etc., 1959-1962. Washington, D.C.: Government Printing Office, 1962.

U.S. Department of Health, Education and Welfare. Food and Drug
Administration. Proceedings of the FDA Conference on the Kefauver-
Harris Drug Amendments and Proposed Regulations, February 15,
1963. Washington, D.C.: Government Printing Office, 1963.

_____. Public Health Service. National Institutes of
Health. Division of General Medical Sciences. Clinical Research
Centers Branch. Procedures and Policies of General Clinical Research
Centers. Washington, D.C.: Government Printing Office, 1962.

_____. Public Health Service. National Institutes of
Health. Group Consideration of Clinical Research Procedures Deviating
from Accepted Medical Practice or Involving Unusual Hazard.
Memorandum, November 17, 1953. Washington, D.C.: Government
Printing Office, 1953.

_____. Public Health Service. National Institutes of
Health. Handbook on Utilization of Normal Volunteers in the Clinical
Center. Washington, D.C.: Government Printing Office, 1961.

_____. Public Health Service. National Institutes of
Health. Healthy Volunteers Help Scientists Conquer Disease. Public
Health Service Publication No. 714, 1959. Washington, D.C.:
Government Printing Office, 1959.

Wood, Robert Caldwell. Ethics in Government As a Problem in
Executive Management. Indianapolis: Bobbs-Merrill, 1955.

State Government

"Ethics Code Becomes Law in New York State." National Municipal
Review (May 1954): 246.

Illinois. Governor. Governor's Ethics Code. Springfield: Governor
of Illinois, 1967.

-62-

_____. State. Ethical Standards in Illinois State Government: Report of the Conflict of Interest Laws Commission. Illinois Legislative Council, 1967.

"Legislative Reform Progresses in New York." National Civic Review 48 (March 1959): 132.

Minnesota. Governor's Committee on Ethics in Government to Governor Freeman. A Report on Ethics in Government. Minneapolis: Governor's Committee on Ethics in Government, 1959.

Moneypenny, P. "The Control of Ethical Standards in the Public Service," in Public Aid in Illinois. Chicago: Public Aid Commission, 1956.

New York. State. Report of the Special Committee on Ethics. Albany: State of New York, 1964.

_____. State. Report of the Special Legislative Committee on Integrity and Ethical Standards in Government. Albany: State of New York, 1954.

_____. State Legislature. Senate. Committee on Ethics and Guidance. Legislative Document No. 9. Albany: New York State Legislature, 1959.

_____. State Legislature. Senate. Committee on Ethics and Guidance. Report and Digest of Pertinent Statutes and Opinions Relating to Integrity and Ethical Standards in Government. Albany: New York State Legislature, 1955.

_____. State Legislature. Special Committee on Integrity and Ethical Standards in Government. Report to Thomas E. Dewey, Governor, and to the Legislature of the State of New York, March 9, 1954. Albany: Williams Press, 1954.

"Texas Legislature Adopts Code of Ethics." National Municipal Review
(July 1957): 358.

"Texas Seeks to Limit Influence Peddling." National Municipal Review
(June 1958): 281.

Local Government

Arlington County, Virginia. Citizens Commission on Ethics in Government Report. Arlington: Arlington County, Virginia, 1952.

The Citizens League of Greater Cleveland. Report of the 1966-67 State
Legislation Committee. Cleveland, The Citizens League of Greater
Cleveland, 1967.

"Code for Legislators" (editorial). National Municipal Review
(Nov. 1952): 488.

"Credo of a Public Servant." National Municipal Review (June 1951):
293.

Denver, Colorado. Code of Ethics for and Conflict of Interests of
Officers, Employees, and Officials. No. 144. Denver: City
Clerk, 1963.

Dewen, R. P. "Cities in Crisis: New York's Harlem Gets Its Own
BBB Office and a Unique Prevention Program." Merchandising Week
100 (July 8, 1968): 8.

Ethical Conduct: A Model Code for Local Government. Kansas City,
Mo.: Civic Research Institute, 1961.

"Ethics Code Adopted in New York City." National Municipal Review
(May 1959): 421.

"Ethics Made Plain" (editorial). National Civic Review (Mar. 1959): 116.

International City Managers Association. A Suggested Code of Ethics for Municipal Officials and Employees. Chicago: International City Managers Association, 1962.

_____. A Suggested Code of Ethics for Municipal Officials and Employees. Chicago: International City Managers Association, 1962.

Marx, F. M. "Ethics and Local Administration." Public Management 33 (Oct. 1952).

_____. "Ethics in Local Government." National Municipal Review (Oct. 1952): 438.

_____. "New Light on Public Ethics." National Municipal Review (June 1953): 276.

Montgomery County, Maryland. Report of the Committee on Conflicts of Interest. Rockville, Md.: Montgomery County, 1959.

New Haven, Connecticut. Code of Ethics. New Haven: New Haven, Connecticut, 1961.

New York City Council. Report on Committee on Ethics and Standards. New York: New York City Council, 1958.

Philadelphia, Pennsylvania. Standards of Conduct and Ethics. Chapter 20-600. Philadelphia: Philadelphia, Pennsylvania, 1963.

Salem, Oregon. An Ordinance Adopting a Code of Ethics for the Public Service in the City of Salem. No. 5633. Salem: Salem, Oregon, 1952.

Politics and Political Philosophy

Adler, Mortimer Jerome. A Dialectic of Morals: Toward the Foundations of Political Philosophy. New York: Frederick Ungar, 1958.

Bailey, Stephen Kemp. Ethics and the Politician: An Occasional Paper on the Role of the Political Process in the Free Society. Santa Barbara, Calif.: Center for the Study of Democratic Institutions, 1960.

Catlin, George Edward Gordon. The Science and Method of Politics. Hamden, Conn.: Anchor Books, 1964.

Deakin, James. The Lobbyists. Washington, D.C.: Public Affairs Press, 1966.

Eccles, David McAdam. Life and Politics: A Moral Diagnosis. London: Longmans, 1967.

Goldwater, Barry. The Conscience of a Conservative. Shepherdsville, Ky.: Victor Publishing Co., 1960.

Gordis, Robert. Politics and Ethics. Santa Barbara, Calif.: Center for the Study of Democratic Institutions, 1961.

Graham, George A. Morality in American Politics. New York: Random House, 1952.

Kaplan, Abraham. American Ethics and Public Policy. New York: Oxford University Press, 1963.

Khann, Herman Richard. Luther's Political Ethics: An Investigation of His Principles. New York: Columbia University Press, 1951.

Leys, Wayne Albert Risser. Ethics for Policy Decisions: The Art of Asking Deliberative Questions. New York: Prentice-Hall, 1952.

Mitler, William Lee. Piety Along the Potomac: Notes on Politics and Morals in the Fifties. Boston: Houghton Mifflin, 1969.

Niebuhr, Reinhold. Moral Man and Immoral Society: A Study in Ethics and Politics. New York: Scribner, 1960.

Nixon, H. C. "Ethics and Politics." Public Administration Review 12 (autumn, 1952).

Reed, Haines Wadsworth. The Morals of Citizenship. Kelvin, Ariz.: Reed Publications, 1954.

Romaine, Howard MacArthur. Consent and Political Obligation. Charlottesville, Va.: Howard MacArthur Romaine, 1967.

Rousse, Thomas Andrew, ed. Political Ethics and the Voter. New York: H. W. Wilson, 1957.

Russell, Bertrand. Human Society in Ethics and Politics. New York: Simon & Schuster, 1955.

"Taking the Curse off Politics" (editorial). National Municipal Review (July 1952): 332.

U.N. General Assembly. Article Seven, Draft Covenant of Civil and Political Rights. New York: United Nations, 1958.

The Utilitarian. "An Introduction to the Principles of Morals and Legislation," by Jeremy Bentham. "Utilitarianism" and "On Liberty" by John Stuart Mill. Garden City, N.Y.: Doubleday, 1961.

Von Eckardt, Ursula Maria. The Pursuit of Happiness in the Democratic Creed: An Analysis of Political Ethics. New York: Praeger, 1959.

Voorhis, Horace Jeremiah. The Christian in Politics. New York: Association Press, 1951.

Wallas, Graham. Human Nature in Politics. Lincoln: University of Nebraska Press, 1962.

Woods, Perry M. The Statesman and the Politician. New York: Pageant Press, 1959.

Wright, Jim, et al. Congress and Conscience. Ed. John B. Anderson. Philadelphia: Lippincott, 1970.

HEALTH SCIENCES

Bibliographies and References

American College of Hospital Administrators and American Hospital
Association. Code of Ethics. Chicago: American College of Hospital
Administrators & American Hospital Association, 1969.

American Hospital Association. Board of Trustee. "Statement of
Principles Involved in the Use of Investigational Drugs in Hospitals."
Journal of the American Hospital Association 31 (Dec. 1, 1957):
106-108.

American Medical Association. Judicial Council. Opinions and Reports
of the Judicial Council of the American Medical Association. Chicago:
American Medical Association, 1960.

_____. Law Department. Medicolegal Forms with
Legal Analysis. Chicago: American Medical Association, 1961.

_____. Opinions and Reports of the Judicial Council.
Chicago: American Medical Association, 1969.
        Elucidation of the principles of medical ethics.

_____. Opinions and Reports of the Judicial Council,
Including the Jurisdiction and Rules of the Judicial Council. Chicago:
American Medical Association, 1966.

_____. Principles of Medical Ethics of the A.M.A.
Chicago: American Medical Association, 1949, 1970.

Catholic Hospital Association of the United States and Canada.
Ethical and Religious Directives for Catholic Hospitals. 2nd ed.
St. Louis: Catholic Hospital Association, 1955.

Curran, W. J. Law and Medicine: Text and Source Materials on Medico-
legal Problems. Boston: Little, Brown, 1960.

Ladimer, Irving. Clinical Investigation in Medicine: Legal, Ethical
and Moral Aspects, An Anthology and Bibliography. Ed. Irving
Ladimer and Roger W. Newman. Boston: Law-Medicine Research
Institute, Boston University, 1963.
    Outstanding study of ethics in clinical investigation, with compre-
hensive bibliography.

Medicine

Abbott, W. O. "The Problem of the Professional Guinea Pig," Trans-
actions of the American Clinical and Climatological Association 68
(1956): 1-9.

Albee, G. W., and R. M. Hamlin. "The Place of Judgment in Clinical
Research." Journal of Clinical Psychopathology 11 (1950): 174-77.

Albert, M. L. "Vietnam: The Doctor's Dilemma." Nation 206 (June 24,
1968): 823-24.
    By virtue of their dedication to preservation of life, doctors
qualify for conscientious objector status in war situations.

Alderman, M. "Medical Experiments of Humans: New Guidelines."
New Republic 155 (Dec. 3, 1966): 23.
    The Public Health Service is criticized for its stance on bio-
medical human experimentation.

Alexander, Shana. "They Decide Who Lives, Who Dies." Life 36
(Nov. 9, 1962): 102-125.
    Shortage of kidney, dialysis machines raises the question of
allocation of treatment priorities, as illustrated at Swedish Hospital,
Seattle.

American Foundation. Medical Research: A Mid-Century Survey.
2 vols. Boston: Little, Brown, 1955.

American Medical Association. "Ethical Guidelines for Clinical
Investigation." Today's Health 45 (Apr. 1967): 70.
     Four major guidelines are listed, based on World Medical
Association and American Medical Association principles.

_____. Law Department: "Responsibility of Physicians
for Use of Research Drugs." Journal of the American Medical Association 158 (1955): 141.

Archambault, G. F. "Investigational Drugs." (editorial). Hospitals,
Journal of the American Hospital Association 32 (1958): 35-36.

Arthur, W. R. "Some Liabilities of the Physician in the Use of Drugs."
Rocky Mountain Law Review 17 (1951): 131-62.

Bailey, N. T. J., and L. J. Witts. "General Principles and Methods,"
in Medical Surveys and Clinical Trials. Ed. L. J. Witts. London:
Oxford University Press, 1959. pp. 12-22.

Barnes, J. M. The Testing of Drugs for Toxicity. Boston: Little,
Brown, 1958. pp. 48-57.

Baron, Paul. Remarks on the Question of Privacy Raised by the
Automation of Mental Health Records. Santa Maria, Calif.: Paul
Baron, 1967.

Barton, R. T. Religious Doctrine and Medical Practice. Springfield,
Ill.: Charles C. Thomas, 1958.

Bauer, R. A. "Risk Handling in Drug Adoption: The Role of Company
Preference." Public Opinion Quarterly 25 (1961): 546-59.

-71-

Bayley, N. "Implicit and Explicit Values in Science as Related to Human Growth and Developments." Merrill-Palmer Quarterly (spring, 1956): 121-26.

Bean, W. B. "The Ethics of Experimentation on Human Beings." in The Clinical Evaluation of New Drugs. Ed. S. O. Waife and A. P. Shapiro. New York: Paul B. Hoeber, 1959. pp. 76-84.

_____. "A Testament of Duty--Some Structures on Moral Responsibilities in Clinical Research." Journal of Laboratory and Clinical Medicine 29 (1952): 3-9.

Beckman, H. "In Defense of Tinkers." New England Journal of Medicine 267 (1962): 72-77.

_____. "To Use the New Drug or Not to Use It--That Is the Question." Journal of the National Medical Association 51 (1959): 83-86.

Beecher, Henry K. "Clinical Impression and Clinical Investigation." Journal of the American Medical Association 151 (1953): 44-45.

_____. "Consent in Clinical Experimentation: Myth and Reality." American Medical Association Journal 195 (Jan. 3, 1966): 34-35.
    Doctors are seen as working for the patient's interests and do not take consent for granted.

_____. "Documenting the Abuses." Saturday Review 49 (July 2, 1966): 45-46.

_____. "Ethics and Clinical Research." New England Journal of Medicine 274 (June 16, 1966): 1354-60.
    Importance of ethical study is reported in the context of twenty-two cases illustrating ethical violations and problems of consent.

_____. "Experimental Pharmacology and Measurement of Subjective Response." Science 116 (1952): 157-62.

_____. Experimentation in Man. Springfield, Ill.: Charles C. Thomas, 1958.
    Coverage includes subjects of experimentation, experimentors, and interrelationships, as well as various legal, moral, and ethical aspects.

_____. Measurement of Subjective Responses:--Quantitative Effects of Drugs. New York: Oxford University Press, 1959.

_____. "The Powerful Placebo." Journal of the American Medical Association 159 (1955): 1602-6.

_____. "Some Fallacies and Errors in the Application of the Principle of Consent in Human Experimentation." (editorial, with comment by W. Modell). Clinical Pharmacology and Therapeutics 2 (1962): 141-46.

_____. "Some Guiding Principles for Clinical Investigation." American Medical Association Journal 195 (Mar. 28, 1966): 1135-36.
    Using general welfare benefits as a welcome goal, the author provides guidelines for human experimentation in some specific examples.

_____. "Surgery as Placebo--A Quantitative Study of Bias." Journal of the American Medical Association 176 (1961): 1102-7.

Bekesy, G. V. "Are Surgical Experiments on Human Subjects Necessary?" Laryngoscope 71 (1961): 367-76.

Beregoff-Gillow, Pauline. A Doctor Dares to Tell: The Inside Story of Medicine. New York: Comet Press, 1959.

Bergin, Richard P. "Law and Medicine--Racial Problems in Medical Practice." American Medical Association Journal 195 (Mar. 21, 1966): 299-301.
This brief considers racial discrimination and problems throughout health-science institutions.

Berkley, Carl. "Ethical Dilemmas in Medical Engineering." American Journal of Medical Electronics 5 (1st quarter, 1966): 9-10.
Recommendation of an ethics committee stems from review of ethical examples in medical engineering experience.

_____. "Opportunities in Medical Engineering." American Journal of Medical Electronics 22 (2nd quarter, 1963): 109-111.

_____. "Technologic Progress and the Hippocratic Oath." American Journal of Medical Electronics 3 (1st quarter, 1966): 1-2.

Bettag, O. L. "Use of Prison Inmates in Medical Research." American Journal of Correction 19 (1957): 4-6, 26.

Beyer, K. H. "Transportation of Drug Studies from Laboratory to Clinic." Clinical Pharmacology and Therapeutics 1 (1960): 274-79.

Biderman, A. D., and J. Zimmer, eds. The Manipulation of Human Behavior. New York: Wiley, 1961.

Bishop, Jerry E. "Ethics, Risks of Experimentation on Human Patients Cause Increasing Concern in the Medical Profession." Wall Street Journal (Aug. 31, 1964): 6.
This article stresses the subtleties of treating sick patients as "healthy" volunteers, with reference to the Nuremberg Code and ethical considerations.

Blasingame, F. J. L. "Comments of American Medical Association--Proposal to Amend Regulations Pertaining to New Drugs for Investigational Use." Journal of the American Medical Association 182 (1962): 932-36.

Bolinger, R. E. "Medical Experimentation on Humans." Science 152 (Apr. 27, 1966): 448.
    The difference between observatorial and manipulative experimentation are dealt with from an ethical viewpoint.

Bonnar, Alphonsus. Medicine and Men. London: Burns & Oates, 1962.

Britain's Medical Research Council to Parliament. "Medical Ethics." Science 145 (Sept. 4, 1964): 1024-25.
    The statement excerpts the procedures of this organization on the specific aspects of human experimentation, aiming at development of a responsible approach.

Bronston, William G. "The Physician and Vietnam." Bulletin of the Atomic Scientists 22 (Nov. 1966): 24.
    Calls for responsibility by doctors during war in recording detrimental effects as an ethical problem.

Bross, Irwin D. J. "Experiment--or Stagnate." New York Times Magazine (July 23, 1967): 4.
    Pointing out some advantages of medieval experimentation, the author discusses superior care devoted to experimental cases and the alternative of lost solutions if experimentation were barred.

Budd, John J. "Medical Ethics--What Is Wrong with Fee Splitting?" Journal of the American Medical Association 195 (Jan. 10, 1966): 117-18.
    A consideration of American Medical Association rulings on fee-splitting cases.

Cahiers Laennec. New Problems in Medical Ethics. Ed. Retio Flood. Trans. Malachy Gerard Carroll. Westminster, Md.: Newman Press, 1953.

Campbell, T. L. "Reflections on Research and the Future of Medicine." Science 153 (July 22, 1966): 442-49.
    The specter of ethics in new genetic developments.

Carley, William M. "Patient Consent to Research; Rules Set." Wall Street Journal (Jan. 21, 1966): 12.
  Review of the Southam v. Mandel case, in which patients were injected with cancerous cells without their knowledge, resulting in the conviction of the experimenters.

Carter, R. The Doctor Business. Garden City,N.Y.: Doubleday, 1958.

[Case] Western Reserve University, Cleveland, Law-Medicine Center. Medical Facts for the Legal Truth. Proceedings of an institute presented by the Law-Medicine Center, Western Reserve University, in cooperation with the Cuyahoga County Coroner's Office, Cleveland, Ohio. Ed. Oliver Schroeder, Jr. Cincinnati: W. H. Anderson Co., 1961.

Ciba Foundation Symposium. Ethics in Medical Progress, London, 1966. Ed. G. E. W. Wolstenholme and Maene O'Connor. Boston: Little, Brown, 1966.

Clark-Kennedy, Archibald Edmund. Man, Medicine and Morality. Hamden, Conn.: Arch Books, 1969.

Claxton, Ernest Edward, and H. A. C. McKay. Medicine, Morals and Man. London: Blandford, 1969.

College of American Pathologists. Committee on Hospital and Institutional Relations. Manual of Contractual and Ethical Relations. Chicago: College of American Pathologists, 1954.

Colloquium on Christian Medical Ethics, 2nd. Concordia Senior College. Proceedings. Ed. Karl W. Linsenmann. St. Louis, Mo.: Lutheran Academy for Scholarship, 1965.

Colloquium on Ethical Dilemmas from Medical Advances, San Francisco. The Changing Mores of Biomedical Research. Ed. J. Russell Elkinton. Philadelphia: American College of Physicians, 1967.

Colloquium on Medical Ethics. Concordia Senior College. Proceedings.
Ed. Karl Kinsenmann et al. St. Louis, Mo.: Lutheran Academy for
Scholarship, 1962.

"Consent Required for Drug Experiments." Science News 90 (Sept. 10,
1966): 172.
    Federal requirements established for patient consent in the use
of investigational drugs.

Cowen, D. L. "Ethical Drugs and Medical Ethics." Nation 189
(Dec. 26, 1959): 479-82.
    Ethical considerations of prescription drug pricing and adver-
tising are discussed.

Crichton, J. M. "Heart Transplants and the Press." New Republic 158
(May 25, 1968): 28-34.
    Questions press involvement in medical operations as an ethical
problem.

Curran, William. "The Law and Human Experimentation." New England
Journal of Medicine 275 (Aug. 11, 1966): 323-25.
    This piece examines consent in experimentation and legal problems
arising from investigational medicine.

_____. "Privacy, Birth Control and Uncommonly Silly Law."
New England Journal of Medicine 273 (Aug. 5, 1965): 322-23.
    Citing a recent law case, this article deals with the constitu-
tionality of birth control practice by individuals.

_____. "Problem of Consent: Kidney Transplantation in
Minors." New York University Law Review 34 (1959): 891-98.
    Another focus on consent problems, this time dealing with
kidney transplants in minors.

Cutler, Donald R. Updating Life and Death: Essays in Ethics and
Medicine. Boston: Beacon Press, 1969.

Damon, V. G. "Fee-Splitting Knife-Happy Surgeons and Mercenary Doctors." Look 26 (June 19, 1962): 86-88ff.
    This decries unethical practices in medicine by certain unscrupulous doctors.

Davidson, Maurice, ed. Medical Ethics: A Guide to Students and Practitioners. London: Lloyd-Luke, 1957.

DeBakey, Michael E. "Medical Research and the Golden Rule." Journal of the American Medical Association 203 (1968): 574-76.
    The author here differentiates between clinicians and practitioners as experimenters, listing guidelines.

Dickel, Herman A. "Medical Ethics--The Physician and the Clinical Psychologist." Journal of the American Medical Association 195 (Jan. 31, 1966): 121-26.
    A comparison and contrast of newer specialists with more traditional physicians.

"Doctors' Dilemma." Scientific American 218 (Mar. 1968): 49-50.
    Covers two major problems in medicine: when to discontinue treatment, and allocation of aid under conditions of limited resources.

Dogliotti, A. M. "Ethical Problems Connected with Surgery." Journal of the International College of Surgeons 34 (1960): 5-7.

Dowling, H. F. "Human Experimentation in Infectious Diseases." Journal of the American Medical Association 198 (Nov. 28, 1966): 997-99.
    The value of continued experimentation is based on past successes such as the contributions in infectious disease treatment by Reed, Jenner, and Harvey.

Edmunds, Vincent, ed. Ethical Responsibility in Medicine--A Christian Approach. Edinburgh: London: E. & S. Livingston, 1967.

Eichenlaub, J. E. "Psychologic Props: The Truth About Doctors'
Deceptions." Science Digest 51 (Feb. 1962): 53-57.
    A critique of psychological treatment of physical ills and
advice for patients.

Elliott, Guy Ambercrombie. Medical Ethics. Johannesburg: Wit-
watersrand University Press, 1954.

"Ethics of Human Experimentation" (editorial). British Medical
Journal 2 (July 6, 1963): 1-2.
    Another review of the Nuremberg Code for Permissible Human
Experiments is the basis for this study of human experimentation
and consent.

Evans, F. J. "New Drugs in Medical Practice: Onus of Experimentation as a Medicolegal Hazard!" Journal of Forensic Science 6
(1961): 10-17.

Fabro, J. A. "Death--What Is at the Heart of It?" National Catholic
Reporter (June 26, 1968): 1, 6.
    Ethical problems of transplant operations.

Ficarra, Bernard Joseph. New Ethical Problems in Medicine and Surgery.
Foreword by Francis J. Connell: Preface by John King Mussio. Westminster, Md.: Newman Press, 1951.

Fink, B. Raymond. "Patient Consent." Anesthesiology 28 (1967):
1109-10.

Finland, Maxwell. "Ethics, Consent, and Controlled Clinical Trial."
Journal of the American Medical Association 198 (1966): 637-38.
    Because of individual disagreement between attending physicians,
an overriding legislative body is inappropriate to decide on the limits
of experimentation on humans.

Finney, Patrick A. Moral Problems in Hospital Practice: A Practical Handbook. Revised and enlarged by Patrick O'Brien. St. Louis, Mo.: B. Herder, 1956.

_____, and P. O'Brien. Moral Problems in Hospital Practice. St. Louis, Mo.: B. Herder, 1956.

Fitts, W. T., and B. Fitts. "Ethical Standards of the Medical Profession." Annals of the American Academy of Political and Social Sciences 297 (1955): 17-36.

Fletcher, Joseph. Morals and Medicine. Boston: Beacon Press, 1960.

Florkin, M. "Medical Experiments on Man." UNESCO Courier 21 (Mar. 1968): 20-23.

Ford, J. C., and J. E. Drew. "Advising Radical Surgery: A Problem in Medical Morality." Journal of the American Medical Association 151 (1953): 711-16.

Forster, F. M. Evaluation of Drug Therapy. Madison: University of Wisconsin Press, 1961.

Fox, R. F. "The Ethics of Clinical Trials," in Quantitative Methods in Human Pharmacology and Therapeutics. Ed. D. R. Laurence. London: Pergamon Press, 1959. pp. 222-29.

Fox, R. C. Experiment Perilous. Glencoe, Ill.: Free Press, 1959.

_____. "Physicians on the Drug Industry Side of the Prescription Blank: Their Dual Commitment to Medical Science and Business." Journal of Public Health and Human Behavior 2 (1961): 3-16.

Franklin, M. A. "Medical Mass Screening Programs: A Legal Appraisal." Cornell Law Quarterly 47 (1962): 205-26.

Franklin, R. K. "Questions of Transplants." New Republic 158 (Mar. 16, 1968): 7.
    Ethical guidelines established in transplant work will ultimately constitute the model for those necessary in genetic experimentation and eugenics.

Fraser, F. "Medical Practice in a Changing Society." Lancet 1 (1958): 154-56.

Freeman, W. "Ethics of Psycho-surgery." New England Journal of Medicine 249 (1953): 778-801.

Freund, Paul Abraham. Experimentation with Human Subjects. New York: George Braziller, 1970.

Furst, W., and W. Furst. "The Medico-legal Aspects of Medical Research." Academy of Medicine of New Jersey Bulletin 5 (1959): 113-18.

Garceau, O. "Morals of Medicine." Annals of the American Academy of Political and Social Science 363 (Jan. 1966): 69-69.
    This discussion covers recent issues and developments in medical ethics.

Gelford, Michael. Philosophy and Ethics of Medicine. Foreword by Sir Robert Aitken. Edinburgh and London: E. & S. Livingston, 1960.

Glorieux, P., and Heger-Gilbert Glorieux. "Some Aspects of Medical Responsibility." World Medical Journal 4 (1957): 298-307.

Gorovitz, Samuel. "Ethics and the Allocation of Medical Resources." Medical Research Engineering 5 (4th quarter, 1966): 5-7.
    Focus in this article is on neglected areas of medical concern, such as resource allocation and differentiation between questions "about" or "of" medical ethics.

Greiner, T. "The Ethics of Drug Research on Human Subjects." Journal of New Drugs 2 (1962): 7-25.

Guenzel, Louis. Medical Ethics and Their Effects upon the Public. Chicago: Louis Guenzel, 1950.

"Guinea Pigs and People." (editorial). Christian Century 79 (Aug. 15, 1962): 975-76.
    Physicians do not have privileges of experimentation on non-consenting patients.

Guttentag, O. E. "The Problem of Experimentation on Human Beings-- the Physician's Point of View." Science 117 (1953): 207-10.

Hadfield, Stephen J. Law and Ethics for Doctors, with a Section on General Practice in the National Health Service. London: Eyre & Spottiswoods, 1958.
    Has sections on negligence contributed by W. G. Hankins and W. Mair; superannuation by L. S. Potler; and income tax by W. Donald.

Harvard Medical School. Rules Governing the Participation of Medical Students as Experimental Subjects. Cambridge, Mass.: Harvard Medical School, 1958.

Harvard University Health Services. Rules Governing Participation of Healthy Human Volunteers and Students in Particular as Experimental Subjects. Cambridge, Mass.: Harvard University Health Services, 1962.

Harvey, J. L. "Control of Drugs by the Food and Drug Administration." Journal of Forensic Science 6 (1961): 1-9.

Hatry, P. "The Physician's Legal Responsibility in Clinical Testing of New Drugs." Clinical Pharmacology and Therapeutics 4 (1963): 4-9.

Hazel, G. R. and H. D. Kautz. "Reporting of Drug Effects and Attitudes of Drug Safety." Current Therapeutic Research 5 (1963): 209-212.

Health Law Center. University of Pittsburgh. "Consent to Medical or Surgical Procedures" in Hospital Law Manual. Pittsburgh: University of Pittsburgh, 1959.

Healy, E. F. Medical Ethics. Chicago: Loyola University Press, 1956.

Heringa, G. C. "The Responsibility of the Medical Press for Medical Ethics." World Medical Journal 2 (1955): 109-110.

Hershey, N. "Problems of Consent in Clinical Investigation," in Report on the National Conference on the Legal Environment of Medical Science. Chicago: National Society for Medical Research & University of Chicago, 1959, pp. 67-69.

Hill, A. B. "Aims and Ethics." in Controlled Clinical Trials. Ed. A. B. Hill. Springfield, Ill.: Charles C. Thomas, and Oxfors: Blackwell, 1960, pp. 3-7.

_____. "Medical Ethics and Controlled Trials." British Medical Journal 1 (1963): 1043-49.

Hollender, M. H. The Psychology of Medical Practice. Philadelphia and London: W. B. Saunders, 1958.

Holman, Edwin J. "Osteopathy and the Law." Journal of the American Medical Association 195 (Mar. 7, 1966): 283-84.
    An outline of relationships between osteopaths, physicians, and hospitals leads to the official American Medical Association position.

Houston Conference on Ethics in Medicine and Technology, 1968.
Who Shall Live: Medicine, Technology and Ethics. Ed. Kenneth
Vaux. Philadelphia: Fortress Press, 1970.

Hubble, Douglas. "Medical Science, Society and Human Values."
British Medical Journal (Feb. 19, 1966).
    Here the doctor is viewed in many roles, particularly as admin-
istrator, investigator, and physician in the framework of human values.

Hyman, W. A. "Medical Experimentation on Humans." Science 152
(May 13, 1966): 856.
    The review concludes that the law denies doctors the right to
experiment without patient knowledge, citing the Southam v. Mandel
case.

Jakobovitz, I. Jewish Medical Ethics. New York: Philosophical
Library, 1959.

Jefferson, G. "Man as an Experimental Animal." Conquest 43
(1955): 2-11.

Johnson, W. H. "The Problem of Experimentation on Human Beings--
Civil Rights of Military Personnel Regarding Medical Care and Experimental Procedures." Science 117 (1953): 212-15.

Karsner, H. T. "Clinical Investigation in Naval Hospitals." Journal
of the American Medical Association 162 (1956): 535-37.

Keaton, H. J. "Malpractice Liability for Medical Experimentation."
California Law Review 40 (1952): 159-65.

Kelly, G. Medico-moral Problems. St. Louis: Catholic Hospital
Association, 1958.

Kelly, W. A. "The Physician, the Patient and Consent." Kansas Law
Review 8 (1960): 405-34.

Kenny, John Pauline. <u>Principles of Medical Ethics.</u> 2nd ed. West-minster, Md.: Newman Press, 1967.

Kerlikowske, A. C., and D. E. Francke. "What Hospitals Should Know About Investigational Drugs--Responsibilities of the Hospital Staff." <u>Hospitals, Journal of the American Hospital Association</u> 32 (Jan. 1, 1958): 45-47.

Kevorkian, J. <u>Medical Research and the Death Penalty.</u> New York: Vantage Press, 1960.

Kidd, A. M. "The Problem of Experimentation of Human Beings--Limits of the Right of a Person to Consent to Experimentation on Himself." <u>Science</u> 117 (1953): 211-12.

"Kidney Transplants." <u>Nature</u> 217 (Feb. 17, 1968): 595.
    This provides brief coverage of legal and moral aspects of kidney transplants, emphasizing consent aspects.

Knock, Frances E. "Ethical Problems of Human Experimentation." <u>American Geriatrics Society Journal</u> 13 (1965): 515-19.
    This argument for a more forceful ethical code uses the field of cancer thermotherapy as a keystone to detailing problems.

Konold, Donald Enloe. <u>A History of American Medical Ethics, 1847-1912.</u> Ann Arbor, Mich.: University Microfilms, 1954.

Lader, L. "Who Has the Right to Live." <u>Good Housekeeping</u> 166 (June 1968): 84-85ff.
    Lack of adequate resources permits saving only 10 percent of appropriate transplant donors, leaving a major problem of selecting those to be saved--in the author's mind a question of public policy.

Ladimer, I. "Ethical and Legal Aspects of Medical Research on Human Beings." <u>Journal of Public Law</u> 3 (1954): 467-511.

_____. "Experimentation: Medical Practice or Malpractice?" World Medical Journal 9 (1962): 207-9.

_____. "Human Experimentation: Medico-legal Aspects." New England Journal of Medicine 257 (1957): 18-24.

_____. "May Physicians Experiment?" International Record of Medicine 172 (1959): 586-98.

_____. "Medical Experimentation: Legal Considerations." Clinical Pharmacology and Therapeutics 1 (1960): 674-82.

_____. "Medical Research on Human Beings," in Report on the National Conference on the Legal Environment of Medical Science. Chicago: National Society of Medical Research & University of Chicago, 1959. pp. 70-77.

_____. "Medico-legal Aspects of Air Pollution Research." Archives of Environmental Health 6 (1963): 772-78.

Langer, Elinor. "Human Experimentation: New York Verdict Affirms Patients Rights." Science 151 (Feb. 11, 1966): 663.
    Illustrates the imposition of experimental regulation and control at New York University.

Lasagna, Lovis. The Doctor's Dilemmas. New York: Harper & Brothers, 1962.

_____. Life, Death & the Doctor. New York: Knopf, 1968.

Lear, John. "Do We Need New Rules for Experiments on People." Saturday Review 49 (Feb. 5, 1966): 61-70.
    The Southam v. Mandel case leads to a recommendation for legal and moral constraints on doctors.

_____. "Research in America: Experiments on People--The Growing Debate." Saturday Review 49 (July 1, 1966): 41-43.
     More on the debate over moral obligations of physicians in human experimentation.

_____. "Struggle for Control of Drug Prescriptions." Saturday Review 45 (Mar. 3, 1962): 35-39.
     This article refers to detailed evidence of ethical violations regarding drug administration.

Logan, Donna. "New Medicine Sires Agonizing Queries." Denver Post-Bonus (Sept. 1968): 5-6.
     Religious reactions to transplant developments is the focus.

_____. "Transplants Moral Issue for Doctors." Denver Post-Bonus (Sept. 1968): 7.
     Surgeons are interviewed on the questions of death and ethical procedure in transplants.

_____. "Transplants: Right or Wrong." Denver Post-Bonus (Sept. 1968): 1-2.
     Again, the issue of transplant work is examined by lawyers, public officials, and surgeons.

Long, R. H. The Physician and the Law. 2nd ed. New York: Appleton-Century-Crofts, 1959.

Loomis, F. "Who Shall Be the Judge?" Readers Digest 86 (Apr. 1965): 91-94.
     Dramatic presentation of argument for continued patient treatment regardless of ultimate prognosis of death.

Lynch, J. J. "Human Experimentation in Medicine--Moral Aspects." Clinical Pharmacology and Therapeutics 1 (1960): 396-400.

McAllister, Joseph Bernard. Ethics with Special Application to the Medical and Nursing Professions. 2nd ed. Philadelphia: W. B. Saunders, 1955.

McCoid, A. H. "A Reappraisal of Liability for Unauthorized Medical Treatment." Minnesota Law Review 41 (1957): 381-434.

_____. "The Care Required of Medical Practitioners." Vanderbilt Law Review 12 (1959): 549-632.

McFadden, Charles J. Medical Ethics. Foreword by Fulton J. Sheen. 3rd ed. Philadelphia: F. A. Davis, 1953.

Markowitz, J., J. Archibald, and H. G. Downie. Experimental Surgery. 4th ed. Baltimore: Williams & Wilkins, 1959.

Marks, J. "Placebomania." Journal of New Drugs 2 (1962): 71-77.

Marley, Faye. "Are Human Tests Ethical?" Science News 90 (Aug. 20, 1966): 115.
    This summarizes recent discussions and declarations of responsibility in human experimentation.

Marshall, John. Medicine and Morals. New York: Hawthorn Books, 1960.

Masters, Norman Chalmers, and H. A. Shapiro. Medical Secrecy and the Doctor-Patient Relationship. Cape Town, South Africa: A. A. Balkema, 1966.

Masters, William H. and Virginia E. Johnson. Human Sexual Response. Boston: Little, Brown, 1966.

"Medical Ethics Debate Boils." Science News 93 (Mar. 23, 1968): 282-83.
    Testimony before a senatorial committee involves heart transplants and medical ethics.

Meyer, Arthur Ernest. Mind, Matter & Morals: The Impact of the
Revolutionary New Findings in Neurophysiology and Psychology upon
the Problems of Religion, Ethics and Human Behavior. New York:
American Press, 1957.

Mills, D. H. "Medical Lessons from Malpractice Cases." Journal
of the American Medical Association 183 (1963): 1073-77.

Mitchell, George. "Heart Association President Probes Transplant
Ethics." Congressional Record 114 (Mar. 11, 1968): 139.
    American Heart Association President Dr. Jesse E. Edwards
discusses heart transplants and ethical problems.

Modell, W. "The Ethical Obligations of the Nonsubject" (editorial).
Clinical Pharmacology and Therapeutics 1 (1960): 137-40.

_____. "Hazards of New Drugs." Science 139 (Mar. 22, 1963):
1180-85.
    In considering new drug development, the extension of applica-
tion to future patients can assist ethical practices and obligations
during the development stage.

Moore, Francis D. "Biologic and Medical Studies in Human Volunteer
Subjects: Ethics and Safeguards." Clinical Pharmacology and Therapeutics 1 (1960): 149-155.

_____. "Ethics in New Medicine: Tissue Transplants."
Nation 200 (Apr. 5, 1965): 358-62.
    A specific recommendation of rules for experimental transplants
calls for more consideration of both patients and corruptibility procedures and tests.

Myers, Maven John. Prescribing Habits of Physicians Who Own
Pharmaceutical Companies. Madison: University of Wisconsin Press,
1966.

Netherlands Public Health Council. "Human Experimentation: Report
Submitted to the Minister of Social Affairs and Health, 1955." World
Medical Journal 4 (1957): 299-300.

-89-

O'Donnell, T. J. Morals in Medicine. Westminster, Md.: Newman
Press, 1959.

Page, I. H. "Medical Ethics." Science 153 (July 22, 1966): 371.
     Doesn't the Hippocratic oath provide individual guidance for
doctors' ethics?

Paget, G. E. "The Safety of New Drugs." Medicine, Science and
the Law 1 (1961): 153-54.

Pappworth, Maurice Henry. Human Guinea Pigs: Experimentation on
Man. London: Routledge & Kegan Paul, 1967.

Parkinson, J. "The Patient and the Physician." Annals of Internal
Medicine 35 (1951): 307-14.

"Patient, Doctor, Human Life." America 103 (July 16, 1960): 451.
     The official Catholic Church position on medical treatment
calls for greater response to patient needs than in the lay areas.

Pesin, Edward, and Ruth Winter. "Organ Transplants: A Legal and
Moral Dilemma." Science Digest 63 (Apr, 1968): 68-72.

Pines, M. "Hospital: Enter at Your Own Risk." McCall's 95
(May 1968): 79ff.

Pius XII. The Moral Limits of Medical Research and Experimentation.
Address to the First International Congress on the Histopathology of
the Nervous System, Sept. 13, 1952. Acta Apostolicae Sedis 44
(1952): 779.

Pius XII. The Prevention of Atomic Warfare, Preservation of Peace,
Medical Ethics, and Human Experimentation. Address to the Eighth
Congress of the World Medical Association, Sept. 30, 1954. Acta
Apostolicae Sedis 46 (1954): 587.

Post, R. H. "Eugenics and the I.U.C.D.'s." Eugenics Quarterly 12 (1965): 112-13.
   Malfunctions of birth-control devices should be researched by a private agency.

Prolongation of Life. Edinburgh: St. Andrew Press, 1960.

"Protecting Human Guinea Pigs." Business Week (July 23, 1966): 71.
   Focus here is on Public Health Service's regulations on research grants.

Pryor, W. J. "Are Medical Ethics an Anachronism." New Zealand Medical Journal 62 (1964): 203-206.
   The history of medical ethics suggests that periodic critical reviews are necessary to keep them applicable to current developments.

Pulvertaft, R. J. V. "The Individual and the Group in Modern Medicine." Lancet 2 (1952): 834-42.

Rackman, E. "Morality in Medico-legal Problems: A Jewish View." New York University Law Review 31 (1956): 1205-1214.

Ramsey, P. "Freedom and Responsibility in Medical and Sex Ethics, a Protestant View." New York University Law Review 31 (1956): 1189-1204.

Randal, Judity. "Merchant Doctors." Reporter 36 (May 4, 1967): 29-30.

_____. "Hearings to Resume on Health Science Commission-- Exhibit 1: 'Naive Howls on Medical Research,'" Congressional Record 114 (Mar. 30, 1968): 46.
   The question of allocating medical treatment should have controls outside the medical community.

Regan, L. J. Doctor and Patient and the Law. 3rd. ed. St. Louis, Mo.: C. V. Mosby, 1956.

Richmond, J. B. "Patient Reaction to the Teaching and Research Situation." Journal Medical Education 36 (1961): 347-52.

Rosenfeld, A. "Search for an Ethic." Life 64 (Apr. 5, 1968): 74-75.
     Another discussion of moral responsibility in transplant work centers on question of rights of doctors not to use transplant under certain circumstances.

Royal Medico-Psychological Association. "The Royal Medico-Psychological Association's Memorandum on Therapeutic Abortion." British Journal of Psychiatry 112 (1966): 1071-73.
     Against legalized abortion, this recommendation calls for traditional medical decision-making in abortions.

Russell, W. M. S., and R. L. Burch. The Principles of Humane Experimental Technique. London: Methuen, 1959.

Sandusk, J. F. "Hazardous Fields of Medicine in Relation to Professional Liability." Journal of American Medical Association 163 (1957): 453-957.

Schiffrin, M. J. "Ethics and New Drugs." Postgraduate Medicine 24 (1958): 305-13.

Schmech, Harold M. The Semi-artificial Man: A Dawning Revolution in Medicine. New York: Walker, 1965.

Schreiner, G. E., and M. D. Bogdonoff. "Limbo to Limb--The Moral and Legal Entanglements of the Clinical Investigator." Clinical Research 11 (1963): 127-30.

Sessoms, S. M. "What Hospitals Should Know About Investigational Drugs--Guiding Principles in Medical Research Involving Humans." Hospitals, Journal of the American Hospital Association 32 (Jan. 1, 1958): 44, 58, 60, 62, 64.

Sheps, M. C., and A. P. Shapiro. "The Physician's Responsibility in the Age of Therapeutic Plenty." Circulation 25 (1962): 299-307.

Shils, Edward, et al. Life or Death: Ethics and Options. Introduction by Daniel H. Labby. Portland, Oreg.: Reed College, 1968.

Shimkin, M. B. "The Problem of Experimentation on Human Beings--The Research Worker's Point of View." Science 117 (1953): 205-207.

Shinners, J. The Morality of Medical Experimentation. Washington, D.C.: Catholic University Press, 1958.

Sidel, V. W. "Medical Ethics and the Cold War." Nation 191 (Oct. 29, 1960): 325-27.
     What is the position of medical confidentiality in national security cases.

Silbermann, M., and J. Ransohoff. "Medico-legal Problems in Psychosurgery." American Journal of Psychiatry 110 (1954): 801-808.

Small, B. F. "Gaffing at a Thing Called Cause: Medico-legal Conflicts in the Concept of Causation." Texas Law Review 31 (1953): 603-59.

Smith, E. E. "Obtaining Subjects for Research." American Psychologist 17 (1962): 577-78.

Sperry, W. L. The Ethical Basis of Medical Practice. New York: Paul B. Hoeber, 1950.

Spitzer, W. O. "Are Heart Transplants Moral?" Christianity Today 12 (Feb. 16, 1968): 24-26.
     Do the criteria governing medical transplants meet societal parameters?

Stetler, C. J., and A. R. Moritz. Doctor and Patient and the Law. 4th ed. St. Louis: C. V. Mosby, 1962.

Strauss, Anselm L. "Medical Ghettos." Trans-Action 4 (May 1967): 7-15ff.
    This report makes a case for improved medical care and services for the poor.

Swetlow, G. I. "What the Law Says About Experimental Therapy." Medical Economics 32 (1954): 181-89.

Taylor, Carl E. "Ethics for an International Health Profession." Science 153 (Aug. 12, 1966): 716-20.
    A call for fuller exchange of information and greater awareness of comparative conditions in the international public health community.

Tenery, Robert M. "Medical Ethics--Medical Etiquette." Journal of the American Medical Association 195 (Mar. 28, 1966): 1137-38.
    This unique approach applies professional courtesy to medical ethics.

Thomson, W. A. R. "Editorial Responsibility in Relation to Human Experimentation." World Medical Journal 2 (1955): 153-54.

Torrey, Edwin Fuller, ed. Ethical Issues in Medicine: The Role of the Physician in Today's Society. Boston: Little, Brown, 1968.

Urquhart, Clara, ed. A Matter of Life. Boston: Little, Brown, 1963.

Vaux, K. "Heart Transplant: Ethical Dimensions." Christian Century 85 (Mar. 20, 1968): 353-56.

Vestal, A. D., R. E. Taber, and W. J. Shoemaker. "Medico-legal Aspects of Tissue Homotransplantation." Journal of American Medical Association 159 (1955): 487-92.

Visscher, Maurice B. "Medical Research and Ethics." Journal of the American Medical Association 199 (1967): 631-36.
    Ethical considerations in vivisection and animal experimentation.

Walpole, A. L., and A. Spinks, eds. The Evaluation of Drugs' Toxicity. Boston: Little, Brown, and London: Churchill, 1958.

Warwick, Warren, J. "Organ Transplants: A Modest Proposal." Wall Street Journal (June 24, 1968).
    A satire on the ethical debate over organ transplants.

"Washington News--Hospital Integration Guidelines." Journal of the American Medical Association 195 (Mar. 28, 1966): 22-23.
    Guidelines are issued to assist hospitals comply with the Civil Rights Act.

Wasmuth, C. E. "Consent to Surgical Procedures." Cleveland-Marshall Law Review 6 (1957): 235-42.

Welt, L. G. "Reflections on the Problems of Human Experimentation." Connecticut Medicine 25 (1961): 75-78.

Wheeler, K., and W. Lambert. "Uneasy Balance, Ethics vs. Profits: Physicians Who Profit from Prescribed Medications." Life 60 June 24, 1966): 86-88ff.
    This proposes drug control legislation to decrease patient vulnerability to unethical medical practices.

Williams, R. H. "The Clinical Investigator and His Role in Teaching, Administration and the Care of the Patient." Journal of the American Medical Association 156 (1954): 127-36.

Witts, L. J. "The Ethics of Controlled Clinical Trials," in Controlled Clinical Trials. Ed. A. B. Hill. Springfield, Ill.: Charles C. Thomas, and Oxford, Eng.: Blackwell, 1960, pp. 8-13.

_____. "Research and the Patient." Lancet 1 (1955): 1115-23.

Wolf, S. "The Pharmacology of Placebos." Pharmacology Review 11 (1959): 689-704.

_____. "Placebos: Problems and Pitfalls." Clinical Pharmacology and Therapeutics 3 (1962): 254-57.

Wolfensberger, Wolf. "Ethical Issues in Research with Human Subjects." Science 155 (Jan. 6, 1967): 47-51.
    Another set of guidelines for all sciences in human experimentation looks at consent, research, and risk concepts.

World Medical Association. "Aspects of Human Experimentation, Special Reports." World Medical Journal 7 (1960): 84-86.

_____. "Principles for Those in Research and Experimentation, Adopted 1954." World Medical Journal 2 (1955): 14-15.

_____, Ethics Committee. "Draft Code of Ethics on Human Experimentation." British Medical Journal 2 (1962): 1119.

Nursing

Catherine de Jesus Christ, Mother. At the Bedside of the Sick: Precepts and Counsels for Hospital Nurses. Trans. E. F. Paeler. Westminster, Md.: Newman Press, 1951.

Dietz, Lena (Dixon). Professional Adjustments. 2 vols. Philadelphia: F. A. Davis, 1950-55.

Hayes, Edward J., et al. Moral Handbook of Nursing: A Compendium of Principles, Spiritual Aids and Concise Answers Regarding Catholic Personnel, Patients, and Problems. Chief moral consultant: Francis J. Connell; chief medical consultants: Samuel A. Cosgrave, Robert Cosgrave. New York: Macmillan, 1956.

LaRochelle, Stanislas, A., and C. T. Fink. Handbook of Medical Ethics for Nurses, Physicians, and Priests. 8th ed. M. E. Poupore, the Rev. A. Carter, and R. M. H. Power. Westminster, Md.: Newman Press, 1949.

Lennon, Mary Isidore, Sister. Professional Adjustments. 3rd ed. St. Louis: C. V. Mosby Co., 1954.

Psychiatry

Bressler, B., et al. "Research in Human Subjects and Artificial Traumatic Neurosis: Where Does Our Responsibility Lie?" American Journal of Psychiatry 116 (1959): 522-26.

Butler, R. N. "Privileged Communication and Confidentiality in Research." Archives of General Psychiatry 8 (1963): 139-41.

Foulds, G. A. "Clinical Research in Psychiatry." Journal of Mental Service 104 (1958): 259-65.

Furst, W., and W. Furst. "The Medico-legal Aspects of Psychiatry Research." Disorders of the Nervous System 21 (1960): 132-34.

Glueck, B. C., Jr. "Research in Mental Hospitals." Mental Hospitals 14 (1963): 93-97.

Kline, N. S., et al. "The Selection of Psychiatric Patients for Research." American Journal of Psychiatry 110 (1953): 179-85.

Perlin, S., and A. R. Lee. "Criteria for the Selection of a Small Group of Schizophrenic Subjects for Biological Studies." American Journal of Psychiatry 116 (1959): 231-43.

_____, W. Pollin, and R. W. Butler. "The Experimental Subject--the Psychiatric Evaluation and Selection of a Volunteer Population." American Medical Association Archives of Neurology and Psychiatry 80 (1958): 65-70.

Rashkin, H. A., and E. R. Smarr. "A Method for the Control and Evaluation of Sociopsychological Factors in Pharmacological Research." Psychiatric Research Reports 9 (1958): 121-30.

Rioch, D. M. "The Application of the Experimental Method of Psychiatric Therapy." Journal of Hillside Hospital 5 (1956): 3-6.

Smith, J. A., and C. L. Wittson. "Hazards of Drug Evaluation: Trials of 84 Non-approved Drugs." American Journal of Psychiatry 117 (1960): 118-19.

Other Health Sciences

American Psychological Association. "Ethical Standards of Psychologists." American Psychology 14 (1959): 279-82.

_____. Ethical Standards for Psychologists. Washington: American Psychological Association, 1953.

American Public Health Association, Committee on Evaluation and Standards. "Clinical Field Cooperative Trials." American Journal of Public Health 53 (1963): 488ff.

Archambault, G. F. "A Drug Moves into Human Trials." Journal of American Pharmacological Association NS3 (1963): 124-27, 136-37.

Arthur, W. R. The Law of Drugs and Druggists. 4th ed. St. Paul: West Publishing Co., 1955.

Berg, T. A. "The Use of Human Subjects in Psychological Research." American Psychology 9 (1954): 108-111.

Bijou, S. W., and D. M. Baer. "The Laboratory-Experimental Study of Child Behavior," in Handbook of Research Methods in Child Development. Ed. P. H. Mussen. New York: Wiley, 1960. pp. 140-97.

Farber, L. H. "Psychoanalysis and Morality." Commentary 40 (Nov. 1965): 69-74.

MacKinney, A. C. "Deceiving Experimental Subjects." American Psychology 10 (1955): 133.

Ohnysty, James. Aids to Ethics and Professional Conduct for Student Radiologic Technologists. Springfield, Ill.: Charles C. Thomas, 1964.

Pellegrino, E. D. "Role of the Hospital Pharmacist in National Therapeutics." Hospitals, JAHA 37 (1963): 102, 105, 107-108.

Rosenstock, I. M., and G. M. Hochbaum. "Some Principles of Research Design in Public Health." American Journal of Public Health 51 (1961): 266-77.

Smith, R. G. "Assuring the Safety of New Drugs." Public Health Reports 71 (1956): 590-93.

Stone, L. J. "Children as Subjects in Psychological Research." American Psychology 10 (1955): 43.

Tattersall, William Richard. The Dentist's Handbook on Law and Ethics. London: Eyre & Spottiswoode, 1953.
    Has sections on forensic dentistry, income tax, and super-annuation by W. R. Tattersall and H. P. Barry, with a section on income tax by W. Donald and a Foreword by E. Wilfred Fish.

Vinacke, W. E. "Deceiving Experimental Subjects." American Psychology 9 (1954): 155.

-99-

Wolkovich, William L. Norms of Conduct for Pharmacists. Clinton,
Mass.: William L. Wolkovich, 1962.

LAW

Legal Codes and Canons

American Bar Association. Canons of Professional Ethics and Canons of Judicial Ethics. St. Paul: West Publishing Co., 1955.

_____. Code of Professional Responsibility and Canons of Judicial Ethics. Chicago: American Bar Association, 1969. Guidelines to ethical practice for lawyers.

_____. Committee on Professional Ethics and Grievances. Informal Opinions. Chicago: American Bar Association, 1969. Official ABA guidelines for district and local grievance groups.

_____. Committee on Professional Ethics and Grievances. Opinions of the Committee on Professional Ethics with the Canons of Professional Ethics Annotated and Canons of Judicial Ethics Annotated. Chicago: American Bar Foundation, 1967. Official digest of rules, procedures, and ethical canons, with citator and index to opinions.

_____. Special Committee on Evaluation of Disciplinary Enforcement. Problems and Recommendations in Disciplinary Enforcement. Final Draft. Chicago: American Bar Association, 1970. A report to the American Bar Association on the state of disciplinary enforcement within the legal profession.

_____. Special Committee on Evaluation of Ethical Standards. Code of Professional Responsibility, Preliminary Draft. Chicago: American Bar Association, 1969.

_____. Statements of Principles with Respect to the Practice of Law. Formulated by representatives of the American Bar Association and various business and professional groups. Chicago: American Bar Association, 1969. Covers law with respect to accountants, architects, bank trust functions, casualty insurers, claims adjusting, collection agencies, life insurance, publishers, realtors, and social workers.

Connecticut Practice. Boston: Boston Law Book Co., 1966.

The Connecticut Practice Book of 1951, A Compilation of Rules and
Forms Pertaining to Civil and Criminal Actions to Take Effect January 2,
1952, Together with the Canons of Professional and Judicial Ethics.
Hartford: Senate of the State of Connecticut, 1951.

New York State Bar Association. Canons of Ethics of the N.Y.S. Bar
Association. Brooklyn: Metropolitan Law Books Co., 1949.

General Law

American Law Students Association. Lawyer's Problems of Conscience.
Chicago: American Law Students Association, 1953.

Bayne, David Cowan. Conscience, Obligations and the Law: The Moral
Binding Power of the Civil Law. Chicago: Loyola University Press, 1966.

Bloom, Murray Teigh. The Trouble with Lawyers. New York: Simon &
Schuster, 1960.

Borkin, J. The Corrupt Judge. Cleveland: World Publishing Co., 1966.

Brand, George Edward, ed. Bar Associations, Attorneys and Judges:
Organization,Ethics, Discipline. Chicago: American Judicature
Society, 1956.

Buehner, Andrew T., ed. Law and Theology: St. Louis, Mo.: Concordia
Publishing House, 1965.
    An address at the dedication of Wessmann Hall, Valparaiso
University, and essays on the professional reponsibility of the
Christian lawyer.

Cahn, Edmond N. "The Lawyer as Scientist and Scoundrel: Reflections on Francis Bacon's Quadricentennial." New York University Law Review 36 (1961): 1-12.

_____. The Moral Decision: Right and Wrong in the Light of American Law. Bloomington: Indiana University Press, 1959.

Campbell, Archibald Hunter. "Obligation and Obedience to Law." British Academy, London, Proceedings 51 (1965): 337-55.

Canales, Josie Tomas. Ethics in the Profession of Law, Containing a Series of Articles on the General Title of Ethics as Applied to Judges and Practicing Attorneys in the Practice of Civil and Criminal Law in Texas. San Antonio: Jose Tomas Canales, 1953.

Carlin, Jerome Edward. Lawyers Ethics: A Survey of the New York City Bar. New York: Russell Sage Foundation, 1966.
    Based on a sample survey of New York City lawyers in private practice, this broad-scale examination implies that legal ethics in actual application often fail to meet standards set by the profession as a whole.

Christensen, Barlow F. Group Legal Services. (Tentative draft.) Chicago: American Bar Foundation, 1967.

Cohen, Felix S. Ethical Systems and Legal Ideas: An Essay on the Foundations of Legal Criticism. Ithaca, N.Y.: Great Seal Books, 1959.

_____. The Legal Conscience: Selected Papers. Ed. Lucy Kramer Cohen. Foreword by Felix Frankfurter; Introduction by Eugene V. Rostow. Hamden, Conn.: Shoe String Press, 1970.

Countrymen, Vern. Problems of Professional Responsibility Under the Uniform Commercial Code. Philadelphia: Joint Committee on Continuing Legal Education of the American Law Institute, American Bar Association, 1969.
    Application of legal ethics and responsibilities of lawyers to situations involving the Uniform Commercial Code.

Dalton, John D. <u>Ethical</u> <u>and</u> <u>Legal</u> <u>Theory</u> <u>in</u> <u>the</u> <u>United</u> <u>States</u>: <u>A</u> <u>Comparative</u> <u>Study</u>. Publication No. 17,223. Philadelphia: University of Pennsylvania, 1956.

Davis, John Denis. <u>The</u> <u>Moral</u> <u>Obligations</u> <u>of</u> <u>Catholic</u> <u>Civil</u> <u>Judges</u>. Washington, D.C.: Catholic University of America Press, 1953.

Donnelly, R. C., J. Goldstein and R. O. Schwarz. "Absolving or Mitigating Circumstances: Problems for Decision Makers at Key Points in the Criminal Process," in <u>Criminal</u> <u>Law</u>. New York: The Free Press of Glencoe, 1962. pp. 61-90.

Drinker, Henry Sandwith. <u>Legal</u> <u>Ethics</u>. New York: Columbia University Press, 1953.
     Comprehensive history of development of the disciplinary arm of the legal profession; guidelines for appropriate legal conduct; and selected official documents and canons as illustrations in the form of appendices.

Durkheim, Emile. <u>Professional</u> <u>Ethics</u> <u>and</u> <u>Civil</u> <u>Morals</u>. Trans. Cornelia Brookfield. London: Routledge & Kegan Paul, 1957.

Feldman, Samuel N. <u>The</u> <u>Student</u> <u>Journalist</u> and <u>Legal</u> <u>and</u> <u>Ethical</u> <u>Issues</u>. New York: R. Rosen Press, 1968.

Freedman, W. "The 1960 Cutter Decision: A Lesson in Judicial Law Making." <u>Defense</u> <u>Law</u> <u>Journal</u> 9 (1961): 19-44.

Fuller, Lon L. <u>The</u> <u>Morality</u> <u>of</u> <u>Law.</u> New Haven: Yale University Press, 1964.

Gingold, Kurt. "Letters--'Captain Levy and the Army System,'" <u>Science</u> 157 (July 14, 1967): 140.
     Military law vs. medical ethics pose the conflict of the rights of citizens in American society.

Hart, Herbert Lionel Adolphus. Law, Liberty and Morality. Stanford, Calif.: Stanford University Press, 1963.

Jenkins, George Raymond. Practice and Legal Ethics with Outline of Study, Lesson Talks and Daily Recitations. Chicago: La Salle Extension University, 1959.

Kalven, J. "A Special Corner of Civil Liberties: A Legal View." New York University Law Review 31 (1956): 1223-37.

Kennedy, H. W. "Legal Aspects of Human Exposure to Atmospheric Pollutants." Archives of Environmental Health 6 (1963): 785-91.

Kevorkian, J. "Capital Punishment or Capital Gain?" Journal of Criminal Law, Criminology and Police Science 50 (1959): 50-51.

_____. Capital Punishment or Capital Gain? New York: Philosophical Library, 1962.

Kindregan, Charles P. The Quality of Life: Reflections on the Moral Values of American Law. Milwaukee: Bruce Publishing Co., 1969.

Lamborn, Leroy L. Legal Ethics and Professional Responsibility: A Survey of Current Methods of Instruction in American Law Schools. Chicago: American Bar Foundation, 1963.

Langer, E. "Court Martial of Captain Levy: Medical Ethics vs. Military Law." Science 156 (June 9, 1967): 1346-50.
    Ethical responsibilities of a physician in the armed forces.

Louisell, D. W., and H. Williams. The Parenchyma of Law. Rochester, N.Y.: Professional Medical Publishers, 1960.

Lund, Sir Thomas George. Professional Ethics. New York: International Bar Association Publications, 1970.
    A guide to professional conduct, ethics, and etiquette of lawyers.

Malone, Rosser Lynn. The Lawyer and His Professional Responsibilities. Lexington, Va.: Washington & Lee University, 1960.

Matthews, Robert Elden. Problems Illustrative of the Responsibilities of Members of the Legal Profession. Cambridge, Mass.: Harvard University Press, 1964.

Mitchell, Basil. Law, Morality and Religion in a Secular Society. London and New York: Oxford University Press, 1967.

Murphy, G. "What Should Be the Relation of Morals to Law?" Journal of Public Law 1 (1952): 313-16.

The Natural Law and the Legal Profession. Chicago: Chicago Bar Association, 1950.
    Lectures delivered under the auspices of the Catholic Lawyer's Guild of Chicago in the headquarters of the Chicago Bar Association.

Northrop, Filmer Stuart Luckow. The Complexity of Legal and Ethical Experience: Studies in the Method of Normative Subjects. Boston: Little, Brown, 1959.

Orkin, Mark M. Legal Ethics: A Study of Professional Conduct. Toronto: Cartwright, 1957.

Petrazhitskii, Lev Iosifovich. Law and Morality. Trans. Hugh W. Babb, with Introduction by Nicholas S. Timashoff. Cambridge, Mass.: Harvard University Press, 1955.

Phillips, Orie L., and Phillbrick McCoy. Conduct of Judges and Lawyers: A Study of Professional Ethics, Discipline and Disbarment. Los Angeles: Parker, 1952.

Pike, James Albert. Beyond the Law: The Religious and Ethical Meaning of the Lawyer's Vocation. Garden City, N.Y.: Doubleday, 1963.

St. John-Stevas, Norman. Law and Morals. New York: Hawthorn Books, 1964.
    Part of the 20th Century Encyclopedia of Catholicism, vol. 148, section 16.

_____. Life, Death and the Law: Law and Christian Morals in England and the United States. Bloomington: Indiana University Press, 1961.

Shklar, Judity N. Legalism. Cambridge, Mass.: Harvard University Press, 1964.

Shuman, Samuel I. Legal Positivism, Its Scope and Limitations. Detroit: Wayne State University Press, 1963.

Smedley, Theodore Allyn. Professional Responsibility Problems in Family Law. Chicago: Council on Education in Professional Responsibility, 1963.

Stone, Julius. Legal Education and Public Responsibility. Columbus, Ohio: Association of American Law Schools, 1959.
    Report and analysis of the Conference on the Education of Lawyers for Their Public Responsibilities, University of Colorado, Boulder, 1956.

Stumpf, Samuel Enoch. Morality and the Law. Nashville: Vanderbilt University Press, 1966.

Tranoff, George. You and Your Profession: A Handbook on Ethics for Illinois Lawyers. Rev. ed. Springfield: Illinois State Bar Association, 1965.

Trumbull, William M. Materials on the Lawyer's Professional Responsibility. Englewood, Cliffs, N.J.: Prentice-Hall, 1957.

Utley, Thomas E. What Laws May Cure: A New Examination of Morals and the Law. London: Conservative Political Centre, 1968.

Virginia General Assembly. Committee on Offenses Against the Administration of Justice. Barratry, Champerty, Running and Capping, Other
Related Offenses and Tax Matters in Connection Therewith, Report.
Richmond: Commonwealth, Department of Purchases and Supplies,
1959.

_____. Committee on Offenses Against the Admin-
istration of Justice. Report to the Governor and General Assembly of
Virginia. Richmond: Commonwealth, Department of Purchases and
Supplies, 1964.

Virginia State Bar. Opinions of Council and Standing Committees on
Legal Ethics, the Unauthorized Practice of Law and Judicial Ethics.
Richmond: Virginia State Bar, 1966.
    Procedural guide for district committees.

Medico-legal Aspects

Adelson, Lester, et al. Physician in the Courtroom. Ed. Oliver
Schroeder. Cleveland: Press of Western Reserve University, 1954.

Hershey, Nathan. The Law and the Nurse. New York: Distributed
by American Nurses Association, 1964.

Kessenich, W. J. "Safe New Drugs and Their Control Under Law."
Clinical Pharmacology and Therapeutics 1 (1960): 53-59.

Lear, John. "Human Guinea Pigs and the Law." Saturday Review 45
(Oct. 6, 1962): 55-57.
    Criticism of drug experimentation abuses and call for govern-
mental regulation by law.

Lessing, L. "Laws Alone Can't Make Drugs Safe." Fortune 33
(Mar. 1963): 123-125, 143-156.

Louisell, D. W. "Legal Limits on Human Experimentation." Archives
of Environmental Health 6 (1963): 784.

Miller, Arthur Selwyn. "Experiments on Humans--Where Are the Lawyers." Saturday Review 49 (July 2, 1966): 48-50.
    Argument for legal responsibility in the establishment of society-wide controls over science and technology in experimental efforts.

"Pathologists--Antitrust and Ethics." Time 43 (July 15, 1966): 52.
    Describes Justice Department suit to establish new ethical standards for pathologists.

Ploscowe, M. "The Place of Law in Medico-moral Problems: A Legal View." New York University Law Review 31 (1956): 1238-45.

Shartel, B., and M. L. Plant. The Law of Medical Practice. Springfield, Ill.: Charles C. Thomas, 1959.

SCIENCE

Bibliographies and References

Auger, P. Current Trends in Scientific Research. Paris: UNESCO, 1961.

Barber, B., and H. Walter, eds. Sociology of Science. Glencoe, Ill.: Free Press, 1962.
　　Readings on the social nature of science and the scientific role, the reciprocal relations between science and society, the organization of scientific work and communication among scientists, the social progress of scientific discovery, and the social responsibilities of science.

Edel, A. "Science and the Structure of Ethics." International Encyclopedia of Unified Science. Foundations of the Unity of Science, 2 (no. 3). Chicago: University of Chicago Press, 1961.
　　This work covers the nature and complexity of the problem; the theory of existential perspectives; and the role of science in conceptual and methodological analysis; decision, freedom, and responsibility.

Freed, J. Arthur. Some Ethical and Social Problems of Science and Technology: A Bibliography of the Literature from 1955. Washington, D.C.: U.S. Department of Commerce, 1964.
　　This bibliography covers the period 1955 to 1963.

Headings, Lois. "Book Notes and Reviews--A White Mouse for the Mines: Moralities for Technopolis II." Business Horizons 10 (summer, 1967): 101-118.
　　List of new books on ethics and certain ethical theories; deals briefly with the particular question of the ethics of the scientist.

Reagan, Charles E. Ethics for Scientific Researchers. Manhattan, Kans.: Kansas State University Press, 1969.

General Works

Adams, Elie Maynard. Ethical Naturalism and the Modern World View. Chapel Hill: University of North Carolina Press, 1960.

Adamson, Arthur. "Letters--the Scientist and the Cominant Danger." Science 133 (Apr. 21, 1961): 1271-72.
    Argues that scientists have no greater ethical responsibility than any other element of our society.

Addinall, R. L. "Cowardly Patient." Science 153 (Aug. 12, 1966): 694.
    The author finds consent forms for medical application would seriously impair medical progress.

Albrecht, William A. "Man and His Habitat: Wastebasket of the Earth." Bulletin of the Atomic Scientists 17 (Oct. 1961): 335-40.
    Man is biologically contaminating himself and all the other populations that support him.

Allison, H. C. "AAAS Defines Social Role of Scientists." Bulletin of the Atomic Scientists 16 (Sept. 1960): 302.

Auger, P. "Scientist Looks at Popularization." UNESCO Courier 15 (June 1962): 14-17.
    The author discusses certain trends relative to the popularization of science.

Baker, B. "Resistance by Scientists to Scientific Discovery." Science 134 (Sept. 1, 1961): 596-602.
    Questions the tenacity of some scientists in holding antiquated views and principles despite new methods and discoveries.

Baker, Jeffrey. "Letters--Science: Philosophical Problems." Science 151 (Feb. 25, 1966): 435.
    Focuses on problems of group subjectivity among scientists and some of its inherent dangers.

Baker, William O. "The Moral Un-Neutrality of Science--Comments." *Science* 133 (Jan. 27, 1961): 261-62.
    Baker holds that since what the scientist may or may not do is determined by "public morality" the scientist must make every effort to gain public trust and understanding.

Beecher, Henry Knowles. *Research and the Individual: Human Studies.* Boston: Little, Brown, 1970.

Bouka, H., ed. *Science and the Future of Mankind.* The Hague, Netherlands: W. Junk, 1961.

Brian, Russell. *Science and Man.* London: Faber & Faber, 1966.

Bronk, D. W. "Idea That Science Can Solve Everything Is a False One." *U.S. News & World Report* 48 (Feb. 22, 1960): 75-76.
    Science is not the end-all to problems, particularly social and political ones.

Bronowski, Jacob. "Moral for an Age of Plenty." *Saturday Evening Post* 233 (Nov. 12, 1960): 24-25.
    The search for truth represents an adequate code of morality for the scientific community.

_____. *Science and Human Values.* New York: Harper & Row, 1965.

Budrys, A. J. "Mind Control is Good, Bad." *Esquire* 65 (May, 1966): 106-109.

Burnham, P. J. "Medical Experimentation in Humans." *Science* 152 (Apr. 22, 1966): 448.
    Satire of consent form derides the argument for firmer control of medical experimentation with human subjects.

Carson, Rachel. The Silent Spring. Boston: Houghton Mifflin, 1962.

Classen, H. George. "Fact and Purpose." Bulletin of the Atomic Scientists 24 (Mar. 1968): 36-38.
    Implicit rejection of ethical values in science based on the premise that the scientific quest for truth is not an ethical end but a basic characteristic of man.

Commoner, Barry. Science and Survival. New York: Viking Press, 1966.
    This work examines many of the ethical problems arising from the technological explosion, citing implications that science may have for controlling research efforts and directions.

Cranberg, Lawrence. "Ethical Code for Scientists." Science 141 (Sept. 27, 1963): 1242.
    Urges consideration of a code of ethics for scientists comparable to that devised by engineers.

_____. "Ethical Code for Scientists." Science 142 (Dec. 6, 1963): 1257.
    Suggests that proposed rules of the Society for Social Responsibility in Science are inadequate as a code of ethics for the Scientific Community as a whole because of limited range of concern of the SSRS.

_____. "Ethical Problems of Scientists." American Scientist 54 (Sept. 1965): 303A-304A.
    Ten examples of ethical problems in science leading to study of the ethical-regulatory system of other professions.

_____. "Ethical Problems of Scientists." Educational Record 35 (summer, 1965): 282-94.
    A case for development and adoption by the scientific community of a professional code of ethics.

_____. "Ethical Problems of Scientists." The Eleventh Edward G. Budd Lecture: Presented at the Franklin Institute, November 2, 1966.

-113-

_____. "An Object of Concern and Study." Virginia Quarterly Review 41 (autumn, 1965): 653-56.
   In the course of a review of Henry Margenau's Ethics and Science, the author contends that there are many serious ethical problems in science that Margenau simply did not deal with.

_____. "Science and Technology--a Time to Respond to the Public Trust," an invited talk given to the Engineering Council for Professional Development: New Orleans, September 30, 1968.
   Seeks to give colleges and universities the responsibility of educating prospective scientists and technologists in ethical awareness and sensitivity.

_____. "Science, Ethics and the Law." Zygon Journal of Religion and Science: 2 (Sept. 1967): 262-71.
   Criticizes scientists for failure to closely examine the relationship of science and ethics, and shows the need for a more formal statement of professional ethical responsibility.

Culliton, B. J. "Consent: It's the Law." Science News 92 (July 22, 1967): 88-89.
   A brief outline of U.S. Food and Drug Administration consent regulations, with an examination of problems arising from the law.

Dam, K. W. "Scientist and Conflict of Interest." Bulletin of the Atomic Scientists 17 (Oct. 1961): 343.

Dash, J. Gregory. "Where Responsibility Lies." Bulletin of the Atomic Scientists 23 (Jan. 1967): 35-37.
   Scientists must recognize responsibility for results of their work, considering the implications during development. Consequences and uses of discoveries are the direct responsibility of those who govern the discovery process, e.g., the atomic bomb.

Dedijer, S. "Research: The Motor of Progress." Bulletin of the Atomic Scientists 18 (June, 1962): 4-7.

_____. "Why Did Daedalus Leave?" <u>Science</u> 133 (June 30, 1961): 2047-52.
    Describes the brain drain of scientific talent from underdeveloped countries to developed ones and the consequences of failure to retain such talent.

_____. "Window Shopping for a Research Policy." <u>Bulletin of the Atomic Scientists</u> 15 (Nov. 1959): 367-71.

DeLeon, Benjamin. "Is Science Morally Sterile?" <u>Bulletin of the Atomic Scientists</u> 24 (May 1968): 54.
    Capitalistic emphasis on science leads to a position of moral neutrality that is implicitly nonscientific in claiming human morality as uncharacteristic of the natural order of man.

DeSolla Price, Derek J. "Ethics of Scientific Publication." <u>Science</u> 144 (1964): 655-57.

Dobzhansky, T. <u>Mankind Evolving</u>. New Haven: Yale University Press, 1962.
    Presentation of the question of intervention in the evolution of mankind by scientific discovery and research, including a discussion of ethical aspects of the situation.

Dubos, Rene. <u>Dreams of Reason: Science and Utopias.</u> New York: Columbia University Press, 1962.

_____. "Scientist and the Public." <u>Science</u> 133 (Apr. 21, 1961): 1207-1211.
    Views the dichotomy of scientist as scientist and scientist as an integral member of society.

DuBridge, L. A. "Science and a Better America." <u>Bulletin of the Atomic Scientists</u> 16 (Oct. 1960): 340.
    The author considers some of the ways in which scientsits can interact more fully with the American society.

Earle, William. "Ethics as Technology." Science 147 (Jan. 8, 1965): 140-41.

Edel, Abraham. Ethical Judgement: The Use of Science in Ethics. Glencoe, Ill.: Free Press, 1955.

Emel'ianov, Vasilii Semenovich. A Scientist's Responsibility. New York: Crosscurrents Press, 1963.

"Ethics of Science Evolved with Man." Science News 89 (Apr. 23, 1966): 229.
    Science provides an evolutionary ethic in permitting man to adapt to his environment and ultimately to exercise control over it.

"Failure to Communicate Seen as Science Crisis." Science News Letter 80 (Oct. 7, 1961): 240.
    Failure to communicate internally and externally is viewed as a major crisis for the scientific community.

Feigl, H., and G. Maxwell, eds. Current Issues in the Philosophy of Science. New York: Holt, Rinehart & Winston, 1961.

Fisher, R. A. The Design of Experiments. 12th ed. Edinburgh: Oliver & Boyd, 1954.

Flora, C. J. "Crantitis." Science 138 (Dec. 7, 1962): 1185-86.
    Concerns ethical standards and abuses of grants given to scientists.

Fosberg, F. R. "Letters--'Code of Ethics.'" Science 142 (Nov. 15, 1963): 916.
    Scientific honesty as the keystone of science represents an adequate code of ethics.

Fozzy, Paula. "Scientists' Social Responsibility." Bulletin of the Atomic Scientists 18 (Mar. 1962): 45-46.
    This news article lists the actions and recommendations of the Committee on Science in the Promotion of Human Welfare of the American Association for the Advancement of Science since 1955.

"French and Japanese Scientists on War Research." Bulletin of the
Atomic Scientists 24 (Mar. 1968): 35.
    Outlines actions of 433 scientists in their appeal to the scientific
community to assume ethical responsibility for its work and to bar use
of that work for destructive purposes.

Fruton, J. S. "Aims and Values of the Sciences." Yale Review 51
(autumn, 1961): 197-210.
    The philosophy of knowledge for the sake of knowledge is
culturally inherent in science, thereby making scientific evolution
a part of the public domain. Corollary to this logic, then: science
is not held responsible for the results of scientific investigation and
discovery.

Gerard, R. W. "Vivisection: Ends and Means." American Institute of
Biological Sciences (now Bio-Science) 13 (1963): 27-29.
    The subject of animal experimentation raises questions concerning
the ethics of objectives and methodology.

Glass, Bentley. "The Ethical Basis of Science." Science 150 (Dec. 3,
1965): 1254-61.
    An argument is made for full disclosure of scientific results,
freedom of inquiry, honesty, and truthfulness as the basis for scientific
ethics.

_____. Science and Ethical Values. Chapel Hill: University of
North Carolina Press, 1965.

Goodman, P. "Human Uses of Science." Commentary 30 (Dec. 1960):
461-72.
    Another proponent of moral neutrality of science applies his theory
on human vs. inhuman uses.

Gray, J. "Science, Man and Society." UNESCO Courier 14 (July,
1961): 30-33ff.

Green, Harold P. "The AEC Proposals--a Threat to Scientific Freedom."
Bulletin of the Atomic Scientists 23 (Oct. 1967): 15-17.
   Opposes regulatory interference with free scientific inquiry.

_____. "The New Technological Era: A View from the Law."
Bulletin of the Atomic Scientists 23 (Nov. 1967): 12-18.
   Undesirable results of certain advances in technology.

Hailsham, L. R. "Imperatives of International Cooperation." Bulletin of
the Atomic Scientists 18 (Dec. 1962): 18.

Harris, Morgan. Cell Culture and Somatic Variation. New York: Holt,
Rinehart & Winston, 1964.
   Ethical problems in connection with scientific probes into somatic,
heredity, and genetic manipulation are set forth in this highly technical work.

Haybittle, John. "Ethics for the Scientist." Bulletin of the Atomic
Scientists 20 (May 1964): 23-24.
   This discussion contends that the individual scientist, not the
scientific community, is subject to ethical considerations and responsibilities.

_____. "Standards of Conduct." Science 136 (June 8, 1962): 9.
   An extension of the case for individual rather than collective
scientific responsibilities.

Heitler, W. "Ethics of the Scientific Age." Bulletin of the Atomic
Scientists 20 (Oct. 1964): 21-23.
   Breakthroughs in certain areas of biology, chemistry, and
technology pose a threat to man and careful, responsible application
of partial knowledge advances is necessary to arrive at the new
ethics for science--respect for life.

Hesburgh, Theodore M. "The Moral Un-neutrality of Science--Comments."
Science 133 (Jan. 27, 1961): 256-61.
   Still another logical examination pointing toward individual ethical
responsibility in scientific work.

_____. "Science and Technology in Modern Perspective."
Vital Speeches 28 (Aug. 1, 1962): 631-34.

Hill, A. T. Ethical Dilemma of Science and Other Writings. New York:
Rockefeller Institute Press, 1960.
        Considers the ethical dilemmas of science under the pressures of
war, politics, and society.

Hirsch, Walter. "Knowledge for What?" Bulletin of the Atomic
Scientists 21 (May 1965): 28-31.
        Calls for scientific responsibility for human welfare as affected
by scientific advances in this age of science, business, politics,
interaction, and pressure.

Hoaglund, Hudson. "Some Reflections of Science and Society."
Bulletin of Atomic Scientists 15 (Sept. 1959): 284-87.
        Describes the acceptance of extended principles of science,
i.e., the search for truth.

John, E. Roy. "The Brain and How It Changes." Bulletin of the
Atomic Scientists 21 (Nov. 1965): 12-14.
        Report on progress in brain research and potential in human
educational processes finds absence of necessary value system a
major obstacle to applications of research.

Johnston, Edgar G., ed. Preserving Human Values in an Age of
Technology. Detroit: Wayne State University Press, 1961.
        A series of lectures by distinguished figures such as Henry
Steele Commager and Francis Biddle.

Kalusler, A. D. "Radiation and Social Ethics." Christian Century
80 (Feb. 13, 1963): 199-200.

Kapitza, P. L. "Future of Science." Bulletin of the Atomic Scientists
18 (Apr. 1962): 37.

Kaplan, Henry S. "Standards of Ethical Conduct." Science 135 (Mar. 16, 1962): 997-98.
    One personal indignant reaction to Soviet resumption of atmospheric atomic testing.

Kemp, John. Reason, Action and Morality. London: Routledge & Kegan Paul; New York: Humanities Press, 1964.

Kenyon, Richard L. "A Lesson from the Lemmings." Chemical and Engineering News 5 (July 15, 1968).
    The increasing impact of technology on our ecology poses a problem in appropriate directions for future technological development.

Kepes, Gyorgy. "The Research Frontier--Where Is Science Taking Us?" Saturday Review 49 (Mar. 5, 1966): 66-67.
    Seeks a balance between technological and artistic values to prevent chaotic situations in our society.

Kety, S. G. "A Biologist Examines the Mind and Behavior." Science 132 (1960): 1861-70.

Kingdon, Frederick. "Letters--'Scientists Indulged,'" Science 145 (Aug. 28, 1964): 873.
    Objection to public tax support of arbitrary pure research based on the whims of certain scientists.

Kubie, L. S. "Some Unsolved Problems of the Scientific Career" (2 parts). American Scientist 41 (1954): 596-613; 42 (1954): 104-112.

Lasagna, L., and J. M. von Felsinger. "The Volunteer Subject in Research." Science 120 (1954): 359-61.

Lanz, Henry. "Letters--'Code of Ethics,'" Science 142 (Nov. 15, 1963): 916.
    Uncodified rules governing science are adequate and followed by most scientists, nullifying any need for a formal code of ethics.

Leach, Gerald. The Biocrats. New York: McGraw-Hill, 1970.

Lear, John. "Morality in Science: Report on a Crisis." Saturday Review 46 (Mar. 2, 1963): 49-54.

_____. "Summons to Science: Apply the Human Equation." Saturday Review 45 (May 5, 1962): 35-39.
    A reminder to scientists that human factors are an important consideration in scientific effort.

Leary, Timothy, et al. "The Politics of the Nervous System." Bulletin of the Atomic Scientists 18 (May 1962): 26.
    The advocates of consciousness-expanding drugs resist attacks on applications of such chemicals as LSD in human subjects.

Lederberg, Joshua. "Experimental Genetics and Human Evolution." Bulletin of the Atomic Scientists 22 (Oct. 1966): 4-11.
    Description of general and specific developments in genetics research and illustrative applications.

Libby, W. F. "Mankind's Adjustment to Scientific Advances." Science Digest 50 (Oct. 1961): 84ff.

Lieberman, E. James. "The Ethical Neutrality of LSD." Bulletin of the Atomic Scientists 18 (June 1962): 41.
    Enumeration of the dangers of LSD and other toxic psychochemicals.

_____. "Psychochemicals as Weapons." Bulletin of the Atomic Scientists 18 (Jan. 1962): 11-14.
    Ethical and physiological objections to the use of a number of psychochemicals as weapons of war.

Lindsay, R. B. "Physics, Ethics and the Thermodynamic Imperative," in Philosophy of Science. Ed. Bernard Baumrin. New York: Wiley, 1963. pp. 411-48.

Lonsdale, Dame Kathleen. "Science and Ethics." Nature 193
(Jan. 20, 1962): 208-214.
Discourse on science as an ethical system and the ethical
role of the individual scientist as a member of society.

MacCoby, Michael. "Social Psychology of Deterrence." Bulletin of
the Atomic Scientists 17 (Sept. 1961): 278-81.
There are ethical reasons for limiting science and technology
as bases for international policy of deterrence.

MacLeish, Archibald. "To Face the Real Crisis: Man Himself."
New York Times Magazine (Dec. 25, 1960): 5ff.
Man's nature is such that he himself, rather than some external
force, presents the main danger to his existence.

McDonald, Donald. "Scientist as Citizen." Bulletin of the Atomic
Scientists 18 (June 1962): 25-28.
Illustrations of scientific reaction to ethical problems.

Margenau, H. Open Vistas. New Haven: Yale University Press, 1961.
Traces recent trends toward human freedom and away from
materialism.

Margolis, H. "Consultants and Conflicts." Science 135 (Jan. 12,
1962): 88-89.
The scientist as consultant may run into some controversial
problems.

_____. "Scientific Advisers." Science 134 (Dec. 1, 1961):
1739.

Mead, M. "The Human Study of Human Beings." Science 133 (1961):
163.

Meade, J. E., and A. A. Parkes, eds. Biological Aspects of Social
Problems. New York: Plenum Press, 1965.
Deals primarily with significant aspects of population trends
from a biological point of view.

Meyer, Herbert M. "The Beginning of the Common-Sense." Bulletin of the Atomic Scientists 22 (Feb. 1966): 23-25.
　　Advocates three-dimensional approach to ethical questions that will integrate personal, scientific, and societal values to provide an overview of the impact of science on social order.

Miller, Cecil. "Human Living--Codes and Problems." Consulting Engineer 17 (Feb. 1967): 110-14.
　　Suggests that professional organizations have formulated soundest solutions to problems of social order and that dedication to simplest precepts may resolve ethical dilemmas.

Miller, D. L. Modern Science and Human Freedom. Austin: University of Texas Press, 1959.

Morrison, P. "Where Is Science Taking Us?" Saturday Review 45 (July 7, 1962): 46.

Muller, H. J. "The Meaning of Freedom." Bulletin of the Atomic Scientists 16 (Oct. 1960): 311-16.
　　Freedom of criticism within the scientific world forms the capstone of scientific ethics.

_____. "Science for Humanity." Bulletin of the Atomic Scientists 15 (Apr. 1959): 146-50.

"New Administration: It Faces a Number of Questions of Scientific Policy: No Easy Solutions in Sight." Science 132 (Nov. 11, 1960): 1382-83.
　　Lists the policy problems facing the incoming political administration.

Oppenheimer, J. Robert. "In the Keeping of Unreason." Bulletin of the Atomic Scientists 16 (Jan. 1960): 18-22.
　　A return to ethical discourse as the regulator of science and technology is the implication of this article.

Panel on Privacy and Behavioral Research. "Privacy and Behavioral Research." Science 155 (1967): 535-38.
    Presidential panel finds that experimentation involving humans must be voluntary, informed, and protective of individual rights and privacy.

Pierce, J. R. "Freedom in Research." Science 130 (Sept. 4, 1959): 450-542.

_____. "The Paper Dragon . . . A Tale of the Times." Physics Today 16 (Aug. 1963): 45-50.
    A satire on the scientific community.

Rabinowitch, Eugene. "Responsibilities of Scientists in the Atomic Age." Bulletin of the Atomic Scientists 15 (Jan. 1959): 2-7.
    Argues for scientific freedom, with the responsibility of educating the public in the uses of science and technology.

Rapport, S., ed. Science: Method and Meaning. New York: New York University Press, 1963.
    This book presents the division of science into its "closed" sense, i.e., nature of scientific activity and research, and in its relationship to the outside world of society and culture.

Rogers, C. R., and B. F. Skinner. "Some Issues Concerning the Control of Human Behavior." Science 124 (1956): 1057-66.

Rostand, Jean. Can Man Be Modified? New York: Basic Books, 1959.

Russell, Bertrand. "The Social Responsibilities of the Scientist." Science 131 (Feb. 12, 1960).

Seaborg, G. T. Freedom and the Scientific Society. Williamsburg, Va.: Colonial Williamsburg, 1962.

Sears, Paul B. "Man and His Habits: The Perspective of Time."
Bulletin of the Atomic Scientists 17 (Oct. 1961): 322-26.
    Our ecological balance is threatened by increases in popula-
tion, technology, and by decreasing consideration of human values
reflected in scientific work.

Shumway, N. E. "State of Many Arts." Science News 93 (Mar. 2,
1968): 213-14.

Sinsheimer, Robert. "The End of the Beginning." Bulletin of the Atomic
Scientists 23 (Feb. 1967): 8-12.
    A case for deeper consideration of change, particularly in
molecular biology.

Sonneborn, T. M., ed. Control of Human Heredity and Evolution.
New York: Macmillan, 1965.
    Publication of a symposium on ethical situations created by
recent biological discoveries and experiments.

Stewart, Bruce. "Science and Social Change." Bulletin of the Atomic
Scientists 17 (Sept. 1961): 267-70.
    Transfer of scientific characteristics of critical analysis to
society are an ethical responsibility.

Teilhard de Chardin, Pierre. The Future of Man. New York: Harper &
Row, 1964.
    Deals with many ethical problems of science as they may bear
upon man's future evolution and development.

Watson-Watt, Robert. "Physicist and Politician." Bulletin of the
Atomic Scientists 15 (Sept. 1959): 298-301.
    The scientist has a special duty as a citizen to communicate
appropriate uses of his scientific efforts.

Weidenbaum, Murray L. "A Matter for the Public to Decide?" Bulletin
of the Atomic Scientists 24 (June 1968): 7.
    Offers society the choice of determining uses of public resources
rather than forcing scientists to enforce internal controls against their
natural inclinations.

Weinberg, Alvin M. "Science, Choice and Human Values." Bulletin of the Atomic Scientists 22 (Apr. 1966): 8-13.
    Applies the criterion of relatedness or wholeness to the choice of scientific research, noting that unity must be merged with the classic search for truth.

Wittenberg, Alexander. "Standards of Ethical Conduct." Science 135 (Mar. 16, 1962): 997.
    Proponent of moral responsibilities and actions for professional scientists.

Wolfe, D. "Research with Human Subjects" (editorial). Science 132 (1960): 989.

Science and Public Policy

Berding, A. H. "Crucial Decade." U.S. Department of State Bulletin 43 (Oct. 31, 1960): 671-76.

Bolt, R. H. "Statesmanship in Science." Physics Today 14 (Mar. 1, 1961): 30-32.

Born, Max. "Physics and Politics." Bulletin of the Atomic Scientists 16 (June 1960): 194-200.
    Continued existence of the world depends on ethical limits considered by scientist and military planners.

Brickman, W. W. "Science, Liberal Arts, and the National Crisis." School and Society 90 (Mar. 10, 1962): 101.

Brode, W. R. "Development of a Science Policy." Science 131 (Jan. 1, 1960): 9-15.
    Relationship of government and science at policy levels.

_____. "Growth of Science and a National Science Program." American Scientist 50 (Mar. 1962): 1-28.

_____. "National and International Science." U.S. Department of State Bulletin 42 (May 9, 1960): 735-39.

_____. "Role of Science in Foreign Policy Planning." U.S. Department of State Bulletin 42 (Feb. 22, 1960): 271-76.
    Necessity for a greater role for science in planning policy.

Bundy, McGeorge. "Scientist and National Policy." Science 139 (Mar. 1, 1963): 805-809.

Bush, V. "Other Fellows' Ball Park." Science 134 (Oct. 20, 1961): 1163.
    Discussion of intrusion of scientists into the areas of politics and government.

Chase, E. T. "Politics and Technology." Yale Review 52 (Mar. 1963): 321-29.
    Political influence of the scientific community and political implications of scientific developments.

"Chemical World 1959/1960; Science in Government." Chemical and Engineering News 38 (Jan. 4, 1960): 63-64.

"Committee of Scholars Support Candidates: Scientists Joining." Science 132 (Oct. 28, 1960): 1238.

DuBridge, L. A. "Policy and the Scientists." Foreign Affairs 41 (Apr. 11, 1963): 571-78.

Etzioni, Amitai. "When Scientists Testify." Bulletin of the Atomic Scientists 20 (Oct. 1964): 23-26.
    Accuses allegedly disinterested scientists testifying before governmental agencies of hiding sociopolitical interests.

Falk, Charles E. "Science and Public Policy Activities in Universities." Bulletin of the Atomic Scientists 24 (June 1968): 50.

Federation of American Scientists. "The War and Weapons in Vietnam." Bulletin of the Atomic Scientists 23 (May 1967): 59-60.
    The opposition to the Vietnam War and a call for restraint of scientific support.

Gilpin, R. American Scientists and Nuclear Weapons Policy. Princeton, N.J.: Princeton University Press, 1962.

Glass, Bentley. "Scientists in Politics." Bulletin of the Atomic Scientists 18 (May 1962): 2-7.

Green, Harold P. "AEC Information Control Regulations." Bulletin of the Atomic Scientists 24 (May 1968): 41-43.

Greenberg, Daniel S. "It's Time for Science to Act Its Political Age." Bulletin of the Atomic Scientists 23 (Oct. 1967): 36-37.
    A proposal to limit military management of research and make science competitive for a share of public funds.

_____. "Science and Foreign Affairs: New Effort Underway to Enlarge Role of Scientists in Policy Planning." Science 138 Oct. 12, 1968): 122-24.

Haskins, C. P. "Technology, Science, and American Foreign Policy." Foreign Affairs 40 (Jan. 1962): 224-43.

Hersh, Seymore M. Chemical and Biological Warfare. New York: Bobbs-Merrill, 1968.

"High Noon in Vermont." Newsweek 58 (Sept. 18, 1961): 92.

Honey, J. C. "Federalist Paper for the 1960's." Saturday Review 43 (July 2, 1960): 43-44.
    Involvement of science in public policy.

Hughes, Thomas L. "Scholars and Foreign Policy: Varieties of Research Experience." Department of State Bulletin 53 (1965): 747-58.
    Role of research in foreign affairs and ethical implications.

Imshenetsky, A. A. "Modern Microbiology and the Biological Warfare Menace." Bulletin of the Atomic Scientists 16 (June 1960): 241-42.
    Russian scientist opposes development of biological warfare capabilities by the scientific community.

Jordan, P., and K. B. Keating. "Scientist in Politics: On Top or on Tap? Summary of Debate." Bulletin of the Atomic Scientists 16 (Jan. 1, 1960): 28-29.

Kennedy, John F. "President Sends Message to Conference on Science and World Affairs." U.S. Department of State Bulletin 45 (Oct. 2, 1961): 533.
    Emphasis on international scientific cooperation.

Killian, J. R., Jr. "Making Science a Vital Force in Foreign Policy." Science 133 (Jan. 6, 1961): 24-25.

_____. "Science and Engineering: Resources for Peace." Bulletin of the Atomic Scientists 18 (Mar. 1962): 2-5.
    Advocates participation of scientists in government to achieve peace.

Kistaikowsky, G. B. "National Policy for Science." Chemical and Engineering News 40 (Jan. 2, 1962): 120-22ff.

Lear, John. "Public Policy and the Study of Man." Saturday Review (Sept. 7, 1968): 59-62.
    Larger role for behavioral scientists is examined.

Levy, L. "Scientists Enter Politics." Science News Letter 78 (Aug. 13, 1960): 106-107.

Moss, John E. "The Crisis of Secrecy." <u>Bulletin of the Atomic Scientists</u> 17 (Jan. 1961): 8-11.
  Early criticism of document classification abuses as an ethical violation of public trust.

Nader, Claire. "The Technical Expert in a Democracy." <u>Bulletin of the Atomic Scientists</u> 22 (May 1966): 28-30.
  Scientists involved in public applications of scientific advances often do not comprehend sociopolitical impact and require greater understanding of common interests.

Pauling, Linus. "Peace on Earth: The Position of the Scientists." <u>Bulletin of the Atomic Scientists</u> 23 (Oct. 1967): 46-48.
  Imperative need seen to educate the public of the threat from further research into nuclear and other weapons.

Steinbach, H. Burr. "Scientists and Public Policy." <u>Bulletin of the Atomic Scientists</u> 18 (Mar. 1962): 10-13.

Szent-Gyorgi, A. "Brain, Morals and Politics." <u>Bulletin of the Atomic Scientists</u> 20 (May 1964): 2-3.

Wittenberg, Alexander. "Ethical Issues." <u>Science</u> 137 (Aug. 10, 1962): 468-69.
  Urges greater role in ethics by professional scientific organizations.

SOCIAL SCIENCES

Bibliographies and References

Albert, Ethel M., et al. A Selected Bibliography on Values, Ethics
and Aesthetics in the Behavioral Sciences and Philosophy, 1920-1958.
Glencoe, Ill.: Free Press, 1959.

American Academy of Political and Social Sciences. Ethical Standards
and Professional Conduct. Ed. Benson Y. Landis. Philadelphia:
American Academy of Political and Social Sciences, 1955.

_____. Ethical Standards in American Public Life. Ed.
Clarence N. Callender and James C. Charlesworth. Philadelphia:
American Academy of Political and Social Sciences, 1952.

_____. Ethics in America: Norms and Deviations. Ed.
James C. Charlesworth. Philadelphia: American Academy of Political
and Social Sciences, 1966.

Church of England. National Assembly. Joint Board of Studies.
Current Problems in the Understanding of Personal Responsibility: A
Bibliography. Westminster, Eng.: Church of England, 1960.

Eppstein, John, trans. and ed. Code of International Ethics. Westminster, Md.: The Newman Press, 1953.

United Nations. Department of Social Affairs. An International Code of
Ethics for Information Personnel: A Short Note on its History and
Development. New York: United Nations, 1952.

Ward, Leo R., ed. Ethics and the Social Sciences. South Bend, Ind.:
University of Notre Dame Press, 1959.
    A collection of essays on ethical approaches to social sciences
by such scholars as Francis G. Wilson, Kenneth E. Boulding, and
Herbert Johnston.

General

Albert, E. M., T. C. Deuise, and S. P. Peterfreund, eds. Great Traditions in Ethics. New York: American Book Company, 1953.
     A collection of classical selections.

Anshen, Ruth Nanda, ed. Moral Principles of Action: Man's Ethical Imperative. New York: Harper & Brothers, 1952.

Baker, Richard Terrill. The Christian As a Journalist. New York: Association Press, 1961.

Baldwin, R. W. Social Justice. Oxford; New York: Pergamon Press, 1966.

Behanan, Mary Thangan (Cherrian). American Justice for Asians: A Case in Point. Gandhinagar: K. T. Behanan, 1955.

Bennett, John C. Christian Ethics and Social Policy. New York: Scribner, 1956.
     This book examines early trends toward a more pragmatic application of morals and ethics to aspects of social life.

Berle, Adolf Augustus, Jr. The Motive Power of Political Economy. New York: Society of Ethical Culture, 1960.

Bourke, Vernon J. Ethics. New York: Macmillan, 1951.

Brandt, Richard B. Ethical Theory: The Problems of Normative and Critical Ethics. Englewood Cliffs, N.J.: Prentice-Hall, 1959.

Breedlove, William, and Terrye Breedlove. The Swinging Set. Los Angeles: Sherbourne Press, 1965.

Brinton, Crane. A History of Western Morals. New York: Harcourt, Brace & World, 1959.
    Survey of the ethical development of the Western World.

Browning, Grayson Douglas. Judgment and Motivation in Contemporary Institutional Ethics. Austin: University of Texas, 1958.

Bryson, Lyman, et al., eds. Symbols and Values. New York: Cooper Square, 1964.
    Significant series of approaches to values over a range of activities in American society.

Cohn, E. N. Moral Decision. Bloomington: Indiana University Press, 1955.

Cook, Fred J. The Corrupted Land. New York: Macmillan, 1966.
    Examination of the pervasive tendency of American society to devalue possession, citing the great electric company scandal and the Billie Sol Estes case as examples of the way in which public attitudes encourage unethical practices.

Cox, Harvey, ed. The Situation Ethics Debate. Philadelphia: Westminster Press, 1968.
    A two-sided view of the important controversy over bringing moral judgment down to individual levels in situational contexts.

Cubbedge, Robert E. Who Needs People? Washington, D.C.: Robert B. Luce, 1963.

Culliton, James W. "Age of Synthesis." Harvard Business Review 30 (Sept.-Oct. 1962): 36-40, 180, 182, 184.

Dasmann, Raymond F. The Last Horizon. New York: Macmillan, 1963.

Durkheim, Emile. Professional Ethics and Civic Morals. London: Routledge & Kegan Paul, 1957.

-133-

Easton, Lloyd David. Ethics, Policy and Social Ends, with Selected Readings. Dubuque, Iowa: William C. Brown, 1955.

"Ethical Standards and Professional Conduct." Annals of the American Academy of Political and Social Sciences, (Jan. 1955 issue).

"Ethics in America: Norms and Deviations." Annals of the American Academy of Political and Social Sciences, (Jan. 1966): 1-126.

Fletcher, Joseph. Moral Responsibility: Situation Ethics at Work. Philadelphia: Westminster Press, 1967.
    An expert application of moral decision-making to such areas as premarital sex, euthanasia, and business management.

Fletcher, Joseph. Situation Ethics: The New Morality. Philadelphia: Westminster Press, 1966.

Gentry, Curt. The Vulnerable Americans. New York: Doubleday, 1966.

God and Caesar: A Christian Approach to Social Ethics. Minneapolis: Augsburg Publishing House, 1959.
    Essays by Walter E. Bauer and others.

Goldstein, Bernice Zinderman. The Changing Protestant Ethics: Rural Patterns in Health, Work, and Leisure. Lafayette, Ind.: Purdue University, 1959.

Goodman, Walter. All Honorable Men. Boston: Little, Brown, 1963.

Gould, Leslie. The Manipulators. New York: David McKay, 1966.

Greenberg, Selig. The Troubled Calling. New York: Macmillan, 1965.

Irwin, William Henry. The American Newspaper. Ames: Iowa State University Press, 1969.

Jacobs, Jane. The Death and Life of Great American Cities. New York: Random House, 1961.

Kazan, Elia. The Arrangement. New York: Stein & Day, 1967.

Leiser, Burton M. Custom, Law and Morality: Conflict and Continuity in Social Behavior. Garden City, N.Y.: Anchor Books, 1969.

Lillard, Richard G. Eden in Jeopardy. New York: Knopf, 1966.

Lippman, Walter. Good Society. New York: Grosset & Dunlap, 1956.
      Introspective optimism applied to man's search for the coexistence of humanism and economic well-being.

_____. Preface to Morals. Boston: Beacon Press, 1960.

Melden, A. I., ed. Ethical Theories: A Book of Readings. New York: Prentice-Hall, 1955.

Messner, Johannes. Social Ethics: Natural Law in the Western World. St. Louis; London: B. Herder, 1965.
      Colossal, detailed examination of societal, political, and economic ethics in their philosophical contexts.

Mumford, Lewis. The City in History. New York: Harcourt, Brace & World, 1961.

Peale, Norman Vincent. Sin, Sex and Self-Control. Garden City, N.Y.: Doubleday, 1965.

Rand, Ayn. For the New Intellectual. New York: Random House, 1961.
      Derisive condemnation of the course set for American society by the priority of materialism among industrial and intellectual leaders.

Rosenberg, Stuart E., ed. A Humane Society. Toronto: University of Toronto Press, 1962.

Ross, Edward Alsworth. Sin and Society: An Analysis of Latter-Day Iniquity. Gloucester, Mass.: Peter Smith, 1965.
    A complaint against increasing complexity in unethical behavior of our society, especially as exhibited by special interest groups.

Saarinen, Aline. The Proud Possessors. New York: Random House, 1958.
    A chronicle of the great American art collectors and the establishment of art as a status symbol.

Sellars, W., and J. Hospers. Readings in Ethical Theory. New York: Appleton-Century-Crofts, 1952.
    Basically a compendium of ethical philosophies and definitions, the final section of this book deals with the general areas of ethics and psychology. The book is pragmatic in emphasis and contains a substantial suggested reading list.

Sleeper, Charles Freeman. Black Power and Christian Responsibility: Some Biblical Foundation for Social Ethics. Nashville: Abingdon Press, 1968.

Smith, Frank E. The Politics of Conservation. New York: Random House, 1966.

Steinbeck, John. The Grapes of Wrath. New York: Viking Press, 1958.

Von Eckardt, Wolf. The Challenge of Megalopolis. New York: Macmillan, 1964.
    Based on the original study of Jean Gottman.

Von Hildebrand, Dietrich, and Alice von Hildebrand. Morality and Situation Ethics. Preface by Bernard Haring. Chicago: Franciscan Herald Press, 1966.

Waddington, Conrad H. The Ethical Animal. London: Allen & Unwin, 1960.

Ward, William G. The Student Journalist and Editorial Leadership. Rev. ed. New York: Richards Rosen Press, 1969.

Weber, Max. The City. New York: Free Press, 1958.

Winter, G., ed. Social Ethics: Issues in Ethics and Society. New York: Harper & Row, 1968.

Wraight, Robert. The Art Game. New York: Simon & Schuster, 1965.
    The author humorously describes some of the unethical games played in buying and selling art objects.

Wright, Dale. They Harvest Despair: The Migrant Farm Worker. Boston: Beacon Press, 1965.
    A narrative account of the maltreatment of migrant workers through-out the Eastern United States.

Wright, Frank Lloyd. The Living City. New York: New American Library, 1963.

Economics

Becker, Gary Stanley. The Economics of Discrimination. Chicago: University of Chicago Press, 1957.

Berle, Adolf A., Jr. Economic Power and the Free Society. New York: Fund for the Republic, 1957.

Boulding, Kenneth E. Beyond Economics: Essays on Society, Religion and Ethics. Ann Arbor: University of Michigan Press, 1968.

_____. "Economics as a Moral Science." American Economic Review 59 (Mar. 1969): 1-12.

_____. The Organizational Revolution: A Study in the Ethics of Economic Organization. Chicago: Quadrangle Books, 1968.

_____. "Religious Foundations of Economic Progress." Harvard Business Review 20 (May-June 1952): 1-8.

Chase, Harold W., and Paul Dolan. The Case for Democratic Capitalism. New York: Thomas Y. Crowell, 1964.

Clark, John Maurice. The Ethical Basis of Economic Freedom. Westport, Conn.: C. K. Kazanjian Economics Foundation, 1955.

Croce, Benedetto. Philosophy of the Practical: Economic and Ethic. Trans. Douglas Ainslie. New York: Biblo & Tannen, 1967.

Ellis, Howard Sylvester. The Economics of Freedom. New York: Harper & Brothers, 1950.

Federal Council of Churches. Christian Values and Economic Life. New York: Harper & Row, 1954.

Frazier, E. Franklin. "The World of Make-Believe," in Black Bourgeoisie. New York: P. F. Collier, 1962.

Friedman, Milton. Capitalism and Freedom. Chicago: University of Chicago Press, 1962.

Fromm, Erich. "Man in Capitalistic Society," in The Sane Society. New York: Rinehart, 1955.

Galbraith, John Kenneth. American Capitalism. Boston: Houghton Mifflin, 1952.

_____. The New Industrial State. Boston: Houghton Mifflin, 1967.

Glazer, Nathan, and Daniel Patrick Moynihan. Beyond the Melting Pot. Cambridge, Mass.: MIT Press, 1963.

Hill, Forest G. "Veblen, Berle and the Modern Corporation." American Journal of Economics and Sociology (July 1967): 279-95.
    Based on a paper presented to the Southwestern Social Science Association at Dallas, Texas on March 27, 1964.

Human Values and Economic Policy--A Symposium. Ed. Sidney Hook. New York: New York University Press, 1967.

"The Influence of Moral and Social Responsibility on Economic Behavior." American Economic Review (May 1961): 527-63.

Journal, Bertand de. The Ethics of Redistribution. Cambridge: Cambridge University Press, 1951.

Keyserling, Leon H. Progress or Poverty. Washington, D.C.: Conference on Economic Progress, 1964.

_____. The Role of Wages in a Great Society. Washington, D.C.: Conference on Economic Progress, 1966.

Knight, Frank. "Economists and Economic Ethics." Ethics 48 (Oct. 1957).

Laulubach, Albert T. Man, Motives and Money: Psychological Frontiers of Economics. Ithaca, N.Y.: Cornell University Press, 1959.

Mannes, Marya. "The Arts: Selling the Public," in More in Anger. New York: Lippincott, 1958.

Munby, D. L. Christianity and Economic Problems. New York: St. Martin's Press, 1956.

Myrdal, Gunnar. American Dilemma. New York: Harper & Row, 1962. 1483 pp.
    Monumental analysis of the great American problem--Negro assimilation into our culture.

_____. Challenge to Affluence. New York: Pantheon Books, 1963.

Obenhaus, Victor. Ethics for an Industrial Age. New York: Harper & Row, 1965.

Ropke, Wilhelm. A Humane Economy: The Social Framework of the Free Market. Chicago: Henry Regnery, 1960.
    Argues a case for injection of other considerations into economic processes beyond traditional demand and supply.

Ross, Arthur M., and Herbert Hill. Employment, Race and Poverty. New York: Harcourt, Brace & World, 1967.

Ruhlen, Ralph Lester. The Relationship of the Economic Order to the Moral Ideal in the Thought of Maritain, Brunner, Dewey and Temple. Ann Arbor, Mich.: University Microfilms, 1959.

Saboderi, Massimo. The Economics of Freedom. New York: Doubleday, 1959.

Seligman, B. B., ed. Poverty as a Public Issue. New York: Free Press, 1968.

West, E. G. Economics, Education and the Politician. Hobart Paper no. 42. London: Institute of Economic Affairs, 1968.

Education

Bernard, Alpha Edgar. The Refinement: Partial Validation of a Professional Beliefs Inventory for Prospective Teachers. Ann Arbor,
Mich. University Microfilms, 1955.

Carpenter, Marjorie, ed. The Larger Learning: Teaching Values and
College Students. Dubuque, Iowa: William C. Brown, 1960.

Cates, Eugene Franklin. What Provisions Have Been Made by Professional Teachers' Organizations for Protecting and Disciplining
Their Members? Ann Arbor, Mich.: University Microfilms, 1958.

Fletcher, C. Scott, ed. Education for Public Responsibility. New
York: Norton, 1961.
        Fourteen reprints of famous articles focused on the requirements
for responsible leadership in our society.

Gauerke, Warren E. Legal and Ethical Responsibilities of School
Personnel. Englewood Cliffs, N.J.: Prentice-Hall, 1959.

Isler, Charlotte. "The Bronx Junior High School Sex Quiz." Saturday
Review 49 (Feb. 5, 1966): 64-65.
        Ethical questions on personality testing of students, illustrated
by lack of parental consent to a sex quiz.

Jones, Betty Mullins. A Code for the Coed. Evanston, Ill.: Alpha
Phi International Fraternity, 1962.

Manwittler, Lloyd V. Expectations Regarding Teachers. Ann Arbor,
Mich.: University Microfilms, 1957.

Mills, Nelson. Factors Affecting the Application of Ethical Principles
by Graduates of State Teachers Colleges of Pennsylvania. Ann Arbor,
Mich.: University Microfilms, 1959.

National Education Association of the U.S. Committee on Professional Ethics. Opinions of the Committee on Professional Ethics with the Code of Professional Ethics, Annotated and an Analysis of the Functions of the Committee. Washington, D.C.: National Education Association, 1955.

_____. Department of Classroom Teachers. Ethics for Teachers. 3rd ed. Washington, D.C.: Department of Classroom Teachers & Research Division, National Education Association, 1958.

_____. National Commission on Professional Rights and Responsibilities. Guidelines for Professional Sanctions. Rev. ed. Washington, D.C.: National Education Association, 1966.

Parry, Thomas Herbert. A Multiple-Choice Test on Ethical Standards in Personnel and Guidance Services. Charlottesville: University of Virginia, 1967.

Piel, Gerald. "Federal Funds and Science Education." Bulletin of the Atomic Scientists 22 (May 1966): 10-15.

Rochester Seminar for Chief School Officers on Ethics and the Superintendency. Ethics and the School Administrator. Ed. Glenn L. Immegart and John M. Burroughs. Danville, Ill.: Interstate Printers and Publishers, 1970.

Wilson, A. G., S. Crockett, A. N. Exto-Smith, and H. Steinberg. "Clinical Evaluation of Effects of Drugs on Medical Students as a Teaching Method." British Medical Journal 2 (1950): 484-88.

History and Narrative Comment

Baruch, Bernard. My Own Story. New York: Henry Holt, 1957.

Batty, Peter. The House of Krupp. New York: Stein & Day, 1967.

Bellamy, Edward. Looking Backward. New York: Random House, 1951.

Clemens, Samuel. "The Man Who Corrupted Hadleyburg," in Complete Short Stories of Mark Twain. Garden City, N.Y.: Hanover House, 1957.

Gibney, Frank. The Operators. New York: Harper & Brothers, 1960.

Harling, John. The Great Price Conspiracy. Washington, D.C.: Robert B. Luce, 1962.

Hewins, Ralph. The Richest American: J. Paul Getty. New York: E. P. Dutton, 1960.

Prothro, James Warren. The Dollar Decade: Business Ideas in the 1920s. Baton Rouge: Louisiana State University Press, 1954.

Sandor, A. "The History of Professional Liability Suits in the United States." Journal of the American Medical Association 163 (1957): 459-82.

Smith, R. A. "The Incredible Electrical Conspiracy." Fortune (Apr. and May 1961).

Stetler, C. J. "The History of Reported Medical Professional Liability Cases." Temple Law Quarterly 30 (1957): 366-83.

Walton, Clarence C., and Frederick W. Cleveland, Jr. Corporation on Trial: The Electric Cases. Belmont, Calif.: Wadsworth, 1964.

Whitney, Simon N. Antitrust Policies: American Experience in Twenty Industries. 2 vols. New York: The Twentieth Century Fund, 1958.

Psychology

American Psychological Association. Casebook on Ethical Standards of Psychologists. Washington, D.C.: American Psychological Association, 1967.

_____. "Social Influences on the Standards of Psychologists." American Psychologist 19 (1964): 167-73.

Bennett, C. C. "What Price Privacy?" American Psychologist 22 (1967): 371-76.

Conrad, H. S. "Clearance of Questionnaires with Respect to 'Invasion of Privacy,' Public Sensitivities, Ethical Standards, Etc." American Psychologist 22 (1967): 356-59.

Dietrich, D. P. "Legal Implications of Psychological Research with Human Subjects." Duke Law Journal, (1960): 265-74.

Freund, P. A. "Is the Law Ready for Human Experimentation?" American Psychologist 22 (1967): 394-99.

Hamblen, John W. "Preservation of Privacy in Testing." Science 151 (Mar. 11, 1966): 1174.
    The author suggests that the use of a computer can efficiently keep test subjects anonymous in certain kinds of psychological testing.

Kanfer, Frederick H. "Issues and Ethics in Behavior Manipulation." Psychology Reports 16 (1965): 187-96.

Katz, M. M. "Ethical Issues in the Use of Human Subjects in Psychopharmacologic Research." American Psychologist 22 (1967): 360-63.

Kline, N. S., ed. Psychological Frontiers. Boston: Little, Brown, 1959.

Krasner, L. "Behavior Control and Social Responsibility." American Psychologist 17 (1962): 199-204.

Levitt, E. E. Clinical Research Design and Analysis in the Behavioral Sciences. Springfield, Ill.: Charles C. Thomas, 1961.

Lovell, V. R. "The Human Use of Personality Tests: A Dissenting View." American Psychologist 22 (1967): 383-93.

McGehee, W. "And Esau Was an Hairy Man." American Psychologist 19 (1964): 709-804.

Mukerjee, Radhakamal. The Dynamics of Morals: A Sociopsychological Theory of Ethics. Introduction by Gardner Murphy. London: Macmillan, 1950.

Nunnally, J., and J. M. Kittros. "Public Attitudes Toward Mental Health Professions." American Psychologist 13 (1958): 589-94.

Ruebhausen, O. M., and O. G. Brim, Jr. "Privacy and Behavioral Research." American Psychologist 21 (1966): 423.
     This case for a code of ethics for the field of behavioral research focuses on definitions of privacy and consent.

Rychlak, J. F. "Control and Prediction and the Clinician." American Psychologist 19 (1964): 186-90.

Schwitzgebel, R. "Electronic Innovation in the Behavioral Sciences: A Call to Responsibility." American Psychologist 22 (1967): 364-70.

Smith, M. Brewster. "Conflicting Values Affecting Behavioral Research with Children." American Psychologist 22 (1967): 377-82.

"Standards of Ethical Behavior for Psychologists." American Psychologist 13 (May 1958): 266-71.
    A report of the Committee on Ethical Standards of Psychologists.

"Surgeon General's Direction on Human Experimentation." American Psychologist 22 (1967): 350-55.

Watson, Goodwin. "Moral Issues in Psychotherapy." American Psychologist 13 (Oct. 1958): 574-76.

Wolfe, Dael. "Psychological Testing and the Invasion of Privacy." Science 150 (Dec. 31, 1965): 1773.
    The author outlines some problems of ethics involved in psychological testing.

Sociology

Borgatta, E. F. "Sociologists and Sociologically Trained Practitioners." American Sociological Review 24 (1959): 695-97.

Fichter, J. R., and W. L. Kolb. "Ethical Limitations on Sociological Reporting." American Sociological Review 18 (1953): 544-50.

Ginsberg, Morris. Essays in Sociology and Social Philosophy. London: Heinemann, 1956.

Handlin, Oscar. The Newcomers: Negroes and Puerto Ricans in a Changing Metropolis. Cambridge, Mass.: Harvard University Press, 1959.
    Comparison of the treatment of earlier waves of immigrants into New York with ethnic groups which have arrived more recently.

Ladd, John. The Structure of a Moral Code: A Philosophical Analysis of Ethical Discourse Applied to the Ethics of the Navaho Indians. Cambridge, Mass.: Harvard University Press, 1957.

Nelson, B. "Anthropologists Overwhelmingly Approve Research Ethics Statement." Science 156 (Apr. 21, 1967): 365.

The Statement on Problems of Anthropolitical Research and Ethics adopted by the Fellows of the American Anthropological Association in April 1967 in part deplores anthropological research as a cover for foreign intelligence activities.

AUTHOR INDEX

Arthur, W. R. 70, 97

Association of Better
Business Bureaus 22

Association of Consulting
Management Engineers 41

Association of the Bar of
the City of New York 57

Auger, Pierre 109, 110

Augustin, Leroy George 51

Austin, Robert W. 2

-B-

Bachrach, Arthur J. 22

Baer, D. M. 98

Bailey, N. T. J. 70

Bailey, Nathan 4

Baker, B. 110

Baker, Jeffrey 110

Baker, Richard Terrill 131

Baker, William O. 111

Baldwin, R. W. 131

Barber, B. 109

Barnard, Chester Irving 2

Barnes, J. M. 70

Baron, Paul 70

Barradell, M. 20

Bartels, Robert 1, 36

Barton, R. T. 70

Baruch, Bernard 141

Batty, Peter 142

Bauer, R. A. 70

Bauer, Walter E. 297

Baum, Maurice 2

Baumhart, Raymond 1

Bayley, H. 70

Baylis, Charles Augustis 51

Bayne, David Cowan 101

Beals, Ralph L. 58

Bean, W. B. 70

Beardsmore, R. W. 51

Beck, K. D. 6

Becker, Gary Stanley 136

Becker, W. C. 42

Beckman, H. 71, 72

Beecher, Henry Knowles 71, 72, 111

Beer, Charles G. 42

Behanan, Mary Thangan 131

Bekesy, G. V. 72

Bellamy, Edward 142

Bennett, C. C. 143

-K-

Kalusler, A. D.	118	Kepes, Gyorgy	119
Kalven, J.	104	Kerlikowske, A. C.	84
Kanfer, Frederick H.	143	Kessenich, W. J.	107
Kapitza, P. L.	118	Kety, S. G.	119
Kaplan, Abraham	65	Kevorkian, J.	84, 104
Kaplan, Henry S.	119	Keyserling, Leon H.	138
Karsner, H. T.	83	Khann, Herman Richard	65
Kattsoff, L. O.	53	Kidd, A. M.	84
Katz, M. M.	143	Killian, J. R., Jr.	128
Kautz, H. D.	82	Kindregan, Charles P.	104
Kazan, Elia	134	Kingdon, Frederick	119
Keating, K. B.	128	Kistaikowsky, G. B.	128
Keaton, H. J.	83	Kittros, J. M.	144
Kefauver, Estes	59	Kline, N. S.	96, 143
Kellogg, Marion S.	34	Knight, Frank	138
Kelly, G.	83	Knock, Frances E.	84
Kelly, W. A.	83	Kolb, W. L.	145
Kemp, John	119	Konold, Donald Enloe	84
Kennedy, H. W.	104	Krasner, L.	144
Kennedy, John F.	128	Krause, Axel	46
Kennedy, Thomas	34	Kresge, Elijah Everett	50
Kenny, John Pauline	83	Kubie, L. S.	119
Kenyon, Richard L.	119	Kuhn, James W.	10
		Kurtz, Paul W.	53

SUBJECT INDEX